Praise for *52 Weeks of Strength for Men*

52 Weeks of Strength for Men is another extension of God's heart as expressed through the gifted writing of Chris Bolinger. Every believer needs a copy of this book – it is a daily invitation to center our emotions and focus our thoughts on the timeless truths of the Bible. I applaud you, Chris, for this outstanding work, and I'm challenged by your devotion to God and His Word. I count it a privilege to walk alongside you in ministry.
—**Craig Fry**, President, Christ Led Communities (CLC)

Men, if you want to learn more about God and integrate the scriptures into your life, this book is the ideal on-ramp. One devotion a week, grounded in the Bible and illustrated with real life stories. Try it – you'll like it.
—**David Murrow**, author of *Why Men Hate Going to Church* and *Drowning in Screen Time*

Having met Chris Bolinger and understanding his great passion to see men grow in Christ, it was so refreshing to see the creative way that *52 Weeks of Strength for Men* so concisely and powerfully captures the transformational way God shapes ordinary men into valiant warriors ready to face each day's battles with God's mighty strength.
—**Richard Buckley**, Regional Vice President, Corporate Chaplains of America

In *52 Weeks of Strength for Men,* Chris hits on the topics all men need to hear. He challenges men to wrestle with life and faith, leading each reader to become a stronger man of God at the conclusion. If all men were to read 52 Weeks, churches would be stronger, families would be healthier, and men would pursue godliness with more fervor. As a pastor, I recommend this resource to all men. This book prepares us like few others to become who the Lord called us to be.

—**Andy Clapp**, author of *Midnight, Christmas Eve, Springtime for Your Spirit,* and *In the Eye of the Storm*

Every week's material has something to think about and discuss. The Bible is central and used sensibly, and the style is accessible and to the point. Most importantly, the topics are ones that make a difference to life.

—**Dr. David Instone-Brewer**, Senior Research Fellow, Tyndale House Cambridge

In *52 Weeks of Strength for Men,* Chris Bolinger begins at the right place, getting our focus on who God is. With Him as our strength, then Chris shares how to tackle everyday big and tough topics men face. Great devotional for those looking for more strength and to dig deeper with the Father!

—**Britt Mooney**, author of *Say Yes: How God-Sized Dreams Take Flight*

As with his previous men's devotional, *Daily Strength for Men,* Chris Bolinger has hit another home run with *52 Weeks of Strength for Men.* Each week's studies are absolute jewels with timeless stories and illustrations both past and present that will touch men where they live. The lessons men learn will bring hope, inspiration and encouragement to be better husbands, fathers and leaders in their churches, places of business and communities.

—**Mark Goldstein**, Central Florida Area Director, CLC

52 Weeks
of Strength for Men

Chris Bolinger

CrossLink Publishing
RAPID CITY, SD

Bolinger/CrossLink Publishing
1601 Mt Rushmore Rd. Ste 3288
Rapid City, SD 57701
https://crosslinkpublishing.com/

Ordering Information:
Quantity sales. Special discounts are available on quantity purchases by corporations, associations, and others. For details, contact the "Special Sales Department" at the address above.

52 Weeks of Strength for Men/Chris Bolinger. —1st ed.
ISBN 978-1-63357-398-7
Library of Congress Control Number: 2021942392

Contents

Pre-Foreword

Kyle Idleman changed my life. Just not in person.

I don't live anywhere near Louisville, where Kyle is the Senior Pastor of Southeast Christian Church. As I write this, Southeast has over a dozen campuses and 25,000 weekly attendees. (It's probably more than that as you read this.) My favorite campus is the Southwest Campus, because people there can say that they attend Southeast Southwest.

Kyle changed my life by writing a book called *not a fan.*, which I read in 2011. I don't remember why I started reading the book but, once I did, I was hooked. I'm not a quick reader, but I raced through *not a fan.* And then I couldn't stop talking about it.

Here's an example. A month or two after I read the book, I had to have a "procedure." I'll spare you the details, except to say that I had a local anesthesia for it. When I'm coming out of a local, I have no short-term memory for about an hour. (The doctor will come into the room and explain the results, and a few minutes later I'll ask whomever is with me, "When is the doctor coming in?" It's hilarious for everyone but me.)

As I recovered from this procedure, I told everyone within earshot about this really cool segment on Nicodemus in *not a fan.* (The well-respected religious leader came to Jesus at night because doing so cost him nothing. Nicodemus believed in Jesus, but he wasn't a follower. He was a fan.) Five minutes after recapping this cool story, I would do it again. For the same audience. I did this about eight times, until they sent me home to entertain my kids with my scintillating story of Nicodemus.

That story, and everything else in the book, hit me right between the eyes. Was I really a follower of Jesus—willing to pick up my cross daily and follow him anywhere, no matter what—or was I a fan? When I took a close look at my life, I couldn't tell. That scared me. What scared me more was the realization that Jesus has no use for fans. Either you're a totally committed follower, or you're on the outside looking in. There's no in-between.

The video series for the book was like a six-part miniseries, with a jarring twist: in the first two minutes, the main character, Eric, drops dead. During the rest of the series, you figure out if he was a fan or a follower. You also see the impact of his life on his wife, his kids, his coworkers, his dad, his childhood friend, and others. Kyle plays one of the characters—Eric's pastor—and narrates throughout the series.

The book challenged me to be a true follower of Jesus. The video series challenged me to put my faith at the front of my life instead of letting it sit in my back pocket. I started by contacting City on a Hill Studio, which created the video series, and asking how I could help. That led to my involvement with two City initiatives: an iPad-based curriculum to teach filmmaking to students and a feature film called *The Song*.

The curriculum never made it to the market. The film was a box office flop; I lost my investment in it. But I gained a lot more. *not a fan.* put me on a different path. A decade later, I'm still on that path. Sometimes I stumble and even fall. Other times, I wander off the path. But God gets me back on my feet and back on the path. Every time. He never gives up on me.

Along the way, I got to meet Kyle and talk with him a few times. I think I thanked him once, but it was one of those lame, "Thanks for all you do!" things that sounds disingenuous. So, when Kyle agreed to write the foreword for this book, it gave me an opportunity to thank him properly.

Kyle, thanks for changing my life.

And for writing the foreword.

Foreword

My dad taught me that the way to get a job done is with the checkbook and a phonebook. (Phonebooks were these paper things that would show up randomly in your mail where you could look up anyone's phone number or find their address.) Well, phonebooks had business numbers in them too, and I don't pretend to know my way around the toolbox, so I especially appreciated that I could find a local expert and pay them to do it.

I know . . . that doesn't really make me seem like the right person to write this foreword. I know men that I would call *men*. They can rebuild the deck in their backyard. They know how to fix the plumbing when there's an issue. When the car starts making a funny noise, they know the problem before the hood is popped. And while I can appreciate them, I am going to go to the mechanic and try to describe the noise.

Some men run into burning buildings and some men don't. But I've learned throughout my life that our strength comes in many forms.

For example, there's a group of men in the church I serve at who recently studied ADA compliance in order to build a wheelchair ramp for a neighbor who desperately needed it. They used a few of their Saturdays and didn't charge the family a penny for the work. Because that's the kind of strength that comes from loving Jesus and your neighbor.

The word *encouragement* means to "speak courage" into someone, and I think this is a season where we need to speak some courage into one another. Most of us think of encouragement as something you give to someone after they do something *worthy* of encouragement, like a "Great work out there!" or a "You knocked it out of the park!"

But that's not what encouragement is. It's what you give to someone ahead of time. You speak courage into him, before he acts. And I think we need more of this kind of strength. The kind of strength that comes from having courage spoken into us, and from speaking it into others.

The best way to begin doing this is to hear what God has spoken to us ahead of time. He's called us to be full of strength and courage. And strength and courage are only as good as what you put your confidence in. Men in the Bible such as Joshua put their confidence in God. You can do the same thing.

I hope that as you pick up this book over the next year God will help you grow in strength and courage no matter what may come your way.

—Kyle Idleman

The Nature
of God

The Bible has two parts: the Old Testament (OT) and the New Testament (NT). In this book, most of the Bible passages are from the NT, so many of them are likely to be familiar. After all, Christians spend most of their time in the NT, even though it's only about 30 percent of the Bible.

When Christians venture into the OT, they sometimes see the God there as, well, a little off-putting. It seems that, if He's not flooding the earth or raining down sulfur, then He's telling His chosen people to slaughter the unchosen. Or demanding sacrifices. Or getting angry about something.

But the God of the OT is the God of the NT. The NT book of Hebrews, written for an audience with a thorough understanding of the OT, makes a compelling case that Jesus is God and then states boldly that "Jesus Christ is the same yesterday and today and forever" (13:8).

So, what is God really like? In this thirteen-week series on the nature of God, you'll see evidence from both the OT and the NT that God:

- Is the **cornerstone** of life
- Is our heavenly **Father**
- Offers us **grace** (God's Riches at Christ's Expense)
- Is **great**, having authority over all things
- Offers us **life** to the full
- Is **light** that breaks through this world's darkness
- Offers us sacrificial **love**, so that we can love Him and others
- Gives **peace** to those who trust in Him
- Is all-powerful, and uses His unlimited **power** for ultimate good
- Is holy and pursues **righteousness** in all things
- Offers us **salvation** through Jesus Christ
- Is the **truth** that transforms lives
- Has an unstoppable **will** to pursue us and bless us

> *For his invisible attributes, namely, his eternal power and divine nature, have been clearly perceived, ever since the creation of the world, in the things that have been made . . .*
> *—Romans 1:20a*

Of all the things that God has made, you are His crowning achievement.

Cornerstone

Bible Passages

1. **Psalm 118** – The rejected stone is the cornerstone
2. **Isaiah 28:16–19** – A cornerstone in Zion
3. **Matthew 7:24–27** – A wise man builds on rock
4. **Luke 20:1–19** – The parable of the tenants
5. **Acts 4:1–12** – Peter and John before the council
6. **Ephesians 2:19–22** – Jesus is the cornerstone
7. **1 Peter 2:4–10** – Jesus is the living stone

"This Jesus is the stone that was rejected by you, the builders, which has become the cornerstone."

—*Acts 4:11*

Shot by a corrupt narcotics officer, Philadelphia detective John Book recovers, and hides, in an Amish community in the 1985 film *Witness*. After he demonstrates carpentry skills, Book is invited to join the rest of the community at a barn-raising. There, every man participates in the building process, with the older and more experienced men providing guidance to the rest.[1]

Amish men know barn-raising . . . and home construction. They develop expertise from personal experience. Some of us do our own home improvements, but home construction? We pay experts to handle that.

In the first century, most men were experts on home construction because they lived in homes that they, or their fathers, had built. The primary building materials were mud bricks reinforced with straw and flat fieldstones. A typical house was a square structure with the bricks or stones layered in courses one story tall, topped by a flat roof of stone slabs stretched across wooden beams.

When Jesus said that a wise man builds his house upon rock and not sand, he was stating the obvious to his audience. The soil in the region around the Sea of Galilee was sandy. During the dry and hot summer, that soil would become hard-baked, almost like concrete. When winter rains came, however, the baked sand could dissipate in a flash, causing everything on it to collapse.

To have a secure foundation for his home, a man would have to dig below the sandy soil until he reached volcanic rock. Using hand chisels, he would dig a trench in the rock, one wide enough to inset the first course of fieldstone or brick.

If there wasn't enough rock for the entire foundation, then he needed at least enough for one corner of the house. There, he would lay the crucial stone in the foundation of any building: the cornerstone. As the first stone set in place, the cornerstone required precise angles and orientation to ensure the structural integrity of the rest of the building.

Jesus was a carpenter by trade but, when he discussed foundations and cornerstones, he wasn't giving advice on home construction. He was talking about life . . . and about God.

The God who had "laid the foundation of the earth" and "laid its cornerstone" (Job 38:4, 6) promised His people that He would lay "as a foundation in Zion, a stone, a tested stone, a precious cornerstone, of a sure foundation" (Isaiah 28:16). David recognized that this vital cornerstone would be one that "the builders rejected" (Psalm 118:22), and Zechariah foretold that it would come from Judah (see Zechariah 10:3-4).

The cornerstone would not be a stone. It would be a man. A man of authority.

Jesus acted with authority, and the religious leaders didn't like it. Shortly after Jesus cleansed the temple, they challenged him in the temple courts. "Tell us by what authority you are doing these things," they said to him. "Who gave you this authority?" Jesus responded by deftly sidestepping that question with a question of his own. Then he told two parables, and the second one answered their question (see Luke 20).

In that second parable, a man plants a vineyard, rents out the land, and goes away. At harvest time he sends a servant to ask the tenants for some of the grapes. The tenants beat the servant and throw him out. The owner sends another servant. Same result. He sends a third. Same result.

Finally, the owner of the vineyard sends his son, whom the tenants surely will respect. But the tenants, recognizing that the son is the heir, kill him. Rather than giving the tenants the inheritance, the owner kills them and gives the vineyard to others.

Jesus finished the parable by citing Psalm 118:22 and adding, "Everyone who falls on that stone will be broken to pieces, and when it falls on anyone, it will crush him."

The answer to the religious leaders' question was this: God gave Jesus his authority. Jesus was the prophesied cornerstone.

Faced with a fundamental challenge to what they believed, the religious leaders responded just as the tenants had: they rejected the Son and killed him.

How will you respond? What kind of life do you want to build?

PRAYER

God, I choose You for the rock on which I build my life. In You I have a core purpose and meaning. You put everything else into plumb when I set my life squarely in You. Direct me to build wisely upon Your strong foundation. Amen.

Questions for Reflection and Application

1. Upon what foundations have you tried to build your life in the past? What happened?
2. In what areas of life do you have the most expertise? Did this expertise come from personal experience or somewhere else?
3. When you have expertise, how willing are you to accept advice or guidance from someone else? From God?
4. Where are you relying on God as your cornerstone the most?
5. Where are you relying on God as your cornerstone the least?
6. What motivates you to make a change in how you approach something?

Father

Bible Passages

1. **Matthew 6:5–15** – The Lord's Prayer begins, "Our Father"

2. **Matthew 7:7–11** – God the Father gives us good things

3. **Mark 14:32–42** – "Abba" is an affectionate term for "Father"

4. **Luke 15:11–32** – The parable of the prodigal son

5. **Galatians 4:1–7** – We are adopted by God as sons

6. **Ephesians 2:11–18** – Through Jesus we have access in the Spirit to the Father

7. **James 1:16–18** – Father of the heavenly lights . . . and you

And because you are sons, God has sent the Spirit of his Son into our hearts, crying, "Abba! Father!" So you are no longer a slave, but a son, and if a son, then an heir through God.

—Galatians 4:6–7

Fathers were the backbone of first-century Jewish society. The father was the spiritual and legal head of his household. He was responsible for feeding, sheltering, and protecting his family. In return, he commanded, and demanded, total respect from his wife and children, even when those children were grown. Older fathers became the revered elders of their community.

Yet when Jesus told a parable in which the father of two sons is the hero of the story, the audience did not respond favorably. They hated the story, because the actions of the father were shocking and appalling to them.

The parable begins with the younger son saying, "Father, give me the share of property that is coming to me." He is telling his father, "You are of no value to me until you are dead and I can get my inheritance. I wish you were dead. In fact, I am treating you as if you were dead. Give me my money now." A good Jewish father would have disciplined and even disowned the son for his incredible disrespect.

Instead, the father in the parable gives the younger son his inheritance without uttering a word.

After that son finds himself destitute in a foreign land, he faces two monumental problems. The first is with his father's community. If it learns that he has squandered his money with non-Jews, the community will have a *Kezazah* (cutting off) ceremony and have nothing to do with him for the rest of his life.

If the son manages to get past the community leaders and make it home, his father will never accept him back into the family. The son's only hope is that the father will take him on as a servant, so he rehearses a speech in which he begs his father to do just that. He knows, of course, that a good Jewish father has every right to reject his plea and send him away. After all, the son had declared his father dead, taken a third of the family's assets, and thrown them away.

Jesus's audience wondered how the father would redeem himself for his humiliating blunder earlier. But the father is just getting started with shameful behavior.

Day after day, rather than focusing on his household, the father scans the horizon for the son who had disrespected and dishonored him. When he spots that son a long way off, the father runs—races—to meet him.

In Jesus's day, a middle-aged Jewish father never ran. Never. He always walked in a slow, dignified manner. To run, he would have to take the front edge of his robes in his hands, as a teenager would. And that would show his legs in what was considered a humiliating posture.[2]

When the father, sweating and out of breath, reaches him, the son starts his well-rehearsed speech about how he has treated his father terribly. The father cuts him off. Will he finally disown this worthless son? No. He does the opposite: he restores him as a son and has a celebration to welcome him back into the family.

The first-century Jewish audience reacted with anger and contempt for the father in the story. But when the audience figured out that the father was a representation of God, they faced a stark choice: reject the teachings of Jesus (and Jesus himself) or rethink everything they thought they knew about God.

But Jesus wasn't done. He finished the story by adding his audience to it, in the character of the older son.

That son hears music from inside the house and asks a servant what is happening. After the servant tells him that the father is throwing a party for the younger son, the older son becomes furious and refuses to go in the house. When his father comes to him, the older son says that he has "served" his father for years and has nothing to show for it, while his wayward brother gets a party.

"All that is mine is yours," the father responds. The story ends.

It turns out that both sons in the story were lost. Both rejected their father.

In the end, only one went to the party.

PRAYER

Heavenly Father, when I am lost, You pursue me. When I turn my back on you, You wait patiently until I come to my senses, and then You welcome me back with open arms. Thank You for calling me Your son. Amen.

Questions for Reflection and Application

1. Only two Old Testament passages refer to God as Father: Isaiah 63:16–17 and Isaiah 64:8–9. Why didn't God's chosen people, the Jews, refer to God as their Father?

2. How did Jews react when Jesus told them that God is their Father? Why?

3. When you think of God as a heavenly Father, what images come to your mind?

4. Describe your relationship with your earthly father. How has that relationship shaped your view of God? Why?

5. When you read the parable of the prodigal son, do you identify with the younger son, the older son, or both? Why?

6. What does it mean to be adopted by God as a son?

Grace

Bible Passages

1. **Psalm 103:1–14** – God is merciful and gracious

2. **Jonah 1:11–2:10** – God sends a fish to rescue Jonah

3. **Joel 2:10–13** – God is slow to anger and abounding in steadfast love

4. **John 3:1–21** – Jesus speaks with Nicodemus

5. **Romans 3:9–26** – We are justified by grace

6. **Romans 5:6–11** – Christ died for us

7. **Titus 3:3–7** – Through Jesus, God pours the Holy Spirit on us

For all have sinned and fall short of the glory of God, and are justified by his grace as a gift, through the redemption that is in Christ Jesus . . .

—*Romans 3:23–24*

One day, the crowd around Jesus was so large that he got into a boat and went just offshore. As he often did, Jesus taught in parables. And, as usual, the parables were odd.

The oddest was about a farmer spreading seed. Rather than spreading the seed evenly on the tilled soil, the farmer threw it everywhere. As a result, some of it landed on the path, some on rocky ground, some among thorns, and some on good soil. Not surprisingly, the only seed that flourished was the last.

Afterward, seeing that his followers were puzzled by this story, Jesus explained that the farmer is God, the seed is the Word, and the four different soils are four different types of people: those easily duped by Satan, those who fall away when trouble strikes, those who care too much about this world, and those who accept the Word and bear fruit.

What Jesus didn't explain is why the farmer throws the seed everywhere. Years later, the person who came to understand why was John Newton.

Newton was born in London in 1725. When he was eleven, his stern sea-captain father took him to sea. After a reckless youth of sea voyages and drinking, Newton was on his way to a position as a slave master on a plantation in Jamaica when he was pressed into the British navy. He attempted to desert, was caught, and received ninety-six lashes. He contemplated murder and suicide. "I was capable of anything," he later recalled.

Granted an exchange to a slave ship bound for West Africa, Newton accepted, and for several years he worked in the slave trade. In 1748, on a return voyage to England, his ship endured a terrible storm. Thinking it might sink, Newton prayed for deliverance. The ship completed its voyage.

A short time later, while on a slave ship bound for the West Indies, he became ill with a violent fever and asked for God's mercy, and again God came through.

The experiences changed Newton's views on God but not the way he lived his life—at least, not initially. He continued to captain slave ships. "I cannot consider myself to have been a believer in the full sense of the word, until a considerable time afterwards," he wrote later.

Only when he suffered a stroke in 1754 did he give up seafaring. Three years later, he applied for the Anglican priesthood, and in 1764 he finally was accepted, becoming a priest at Olney in Buckinghamshire.

Eight years later, Newton wrote a hymn in which he revealed the guilt that he felt about his participation in the slave trade—he was a "wretch" who was "lost" and "blind." In 1788, thirty-four years after leaving the slave trade, he renounced his former profession by publishing the pamphlet "Thoughts upon the Slave Trade," which described the horrific conditions on slave ships. That pamphlet, as well as conversations between Newton and Parliament member William Wilberforce, played a role in Parliament's decision to outlaw slavery in Great Britain in 1807, just before Newton died.

Newton's hymn was "Amazing Grace":

Amazing grace! How sweet the sound!
That saved a wretch like me!
I once was lost, but now am found;
was blind, but now I see...
Through many dangers, toils, and snares
I have already come.
'Tis grace that brought me safe thus far,
and grace will lead me home.[3]

Why does the farmer throw seed on the path? On the rocky ground? Among thorns? He has an unbelievable amount of seed. His bag is endless. He can afford to throw it anywhere and everywhere. Again and again.

And he knows that hard ground, even a path, can be tilled and eventually become soft. Rocks can be removed. Weeds and thorns can be pulled.

The lost can be found. The blind can see. Wretches can be saved.

God's free gift of grace is available to anyone. Even slave ship captains. And you. And me.

PRAYER

Lord, I don't deserve Your grace and mercy, but I sure do need them. Thank You for loving me, even when I screw up, again and again. Spur me to tell others of Your grace, mercy, and goodness. Amen.

Questions for Reflection and Application

1. Some have said that we all go through phases of life where our hearts can be good soil, thorny ground, a hard path, or rocky ground. Do you agree? Why or why not?

2. What kind of soil is your heart right now? If it's not "fertile ground," then what needs to change for it to be so?

3. In the song "Real Good Thing," the band Newsboys explains grace as getting what you don't deserve and not getting what you deserve. What personal experiences of grace does this bring to mind?

4. How did Newton respond to God's grace? How should you?

5. If we are to be like God, then we must extend grace, too. To whom is God calling you to extend grace? How can you do that? What challenges do you face in doing that?

Greatness

Bible Passages

1. **Deuteronomy 11:1–7** – Moses reminds Israel of God's greatness

2. **2 Samuel 7:18–29** – David praises God's greatness

3. **Job 38** – From a whirlwind, God lectures Job on His greatness

4. **Psalm 145:1–9** – God's works show His greatness

5. **Mark 4:35–41** – Jesus calms a storm

6. **2 Corinthians 3:12–18** – We behold God's glory

7. **Ephesians 1:15–23** – God's power is immeasurably great

And the wind ceased, and there was a great calm. He said to them, "Why are you so afraid? Have you still no faith?" And they were filled with great fear and said to one another, "Who then is this, that even the wind and the sea obey him?"

—*Mark 4:39b–41*

Early in the three-year ministry of Jesus, the disciples had a front-row seat to some amazing feats of power. People with all kinds of afflictions—common diseases, disfiguring skin diseases such as leprosy, unclean spirits, paralysis—were brought to Jesus, and he healed every one of them. It was amazing. But it was just a tiny glimpse of the power Jesus wielded.

One evening, Jesus and his disciples decided to cross the Sea of Galilee. A fierce windstorm arose. Waves crashed into the boat, and it began to fill with water. Fearing that the boat would capsize, the disciples woke Jesus, who was asleep in the stern. Jesus rebuked the wind and said to the sea, "Peace! Be still!"

Just like that, everything was calm. And the disciples, who had been afraid of the storm, now were terrified of Jesus. "Who is he?" they asked each other. "Even the wind and the sea obey him!"

Later, they discovered why Jesus was so powerful. He and the Father were one.

Everyone knew that God was powerful. All-powerful. They called Him the God of Angel Armies. But God was more than powerful. God was holy. God was just and fair. God was gracious, and loving, and merciful. So, rather than worshipping God for His power, the Israelites worshipped God for His greatness. In Psalm 145, David describes God's greatness as "unsearchable" and God's deeds as "mighty," "wondrous," and "awesome." God's everlasting kingdom, David writes, is filled with the glorious splendor of God's majesty.

God's greatness is so overwhelming that no one can see God and live. The closest that anyone came to seeing God was Moses, when the people of Israel were camped by Mount Sinai. When Moses asked to see God—or God's "glory"—God responded that He would cover Moses with His hand until He had passed by and allow Moses to see only His "back." Then God gave Moses two stone tablets to replace the two that Moses had broken when he saw his people dancing around a golden calf.

When Moses came down from Mount Sinai, his face shone so brightly that everyone was afraid to come near him. Moses began to wear a veil to reduce the brilliance of the shining. He removed the veil when he spoke to God and then put it back on afterward. When the Israelites constructed the tabernacle as their place of worship, they put a veil over the entrance to the Holy of Holies, where the presence of God was manifested. Once a year, the High Priest was allowed to open the veil, enter the Holy of Holies, and sprinkle blood on the Mercy Seat, the golden lid on the Ark of the Covenant, to atone for the people's sins that year.

In his first letter to Timothy, Paul describes God as "the blessed and only Sovereign, the King of Kings and Lord of Lords, who alone has immortality, who dwells in unapproachable light, whom no one has ever seen or can see" (6:15-16). But in 2 Corinthians, Paul writes that all believers behold the glory of God. How can this be? God has given us a new covenant, writes Paul, not based on the Law but of the Spirit. "But when one turns to the Lord, the veil is removed. Now the Lord is the Spirit, and where the Spirit of the Lord is, there is freedom. And we all, with unveiled face, beholding the glory of the Lord, are being transformed into the same image from one degree of glory to another" (3:16–18).

The prophet Jeremiah spoke about this new covenant to a nation that had broken the old covenant and, as a result, had been taken as captives to Babylon. In the new covenant, God promised to write the law on the hearts of His people. At his final Passover meal with his disciples, Jesus told them that the new covenant was in his blood. That blood, of course, was shed on the cross the next day.

God is great. His greatness is so overpowering that it makes Him unapproachable. So, God sent His Son:

who, though he was in the form of God, did not count equality with God a thing to be grasped, but emptied himself, by taking the form of a servant, being born in the likeness of men. And being found in human form, he humbled himself by becoming obedient to the point of death, even death on a cross! (Philippians 2:6–8)

Jesus gave us glimpses into all the attributes of God, including His greatness. And we are able to approach our great God as Jesus did. As a beloved son.

Face to face.

PRAYER

Our Father, who art in Heaven, hallowed be Thy name. You are great and powerful beyond my comprehension. You alone are God. And yet You love me! Thank You for calling me Your friend and Your son. Amen.

Questions for Reflection and Application

1. Write down adjectives other than "great" that capture some element of God's greatness. For each, think of an example.
2. What is your favorite Bible passage on God's greatness? Why?
3. In the past month, where in your life have you seen glimpses of God's greatness on display?
4. Outside of your own personal experience, where do you see the most examples of God's greatness?
5. If God is so great, then why does He care about us?
6. Does God's greatness make you hesitant to bring minor issues to Him in prayer? Why or why not?

Life

Bible Passages

1. **Genesis 1:20–31** – God creates all living creatures, including people

2. **Deuteronomy 30:11–20** – Choose life in God

3. **Ezekiel 37:1–14** – God brings dry bones to life

4. **John 10:1–10** – Jesus promises abundant life

5. **John 11:21–27** – Jesus is the resurrection and the life

6. **John 14:1–7** – Jesus is the way, the truth, and the life

7. **Romans 6:1–14** – In Jesus, we are dead to sin, alive in God

"I am the door. If anyone enters by me, he will be saved and will go in and out and find pasture. The thief comes only to steal and kill and destroy. I came that they may have life and have it abundantly."

—John 10:9–10

G od created us not just to exist but to have *life*. Rich, abundant life. At the very beginning, in the garden of Eden, we had that. But sin entered, and we were driven from the garden. Since then, we have had a longing to experience life as God designed it.

Sometimes, we get a glimpse of that life, and a renewal of our spirit, through the works of others.

In 1984, the British band Talk Talk had a hit with "It's My Life" (later covered by No Doubt). Talk Talk toured with Duran Duran, and audiences eagerly awaited more synth-pop hits from songwriter Mark Hollis and crew. But Hollis had other ideas.

Talk Talk's third album, *The Colour of Spring*, had a dramatically different style, with complicated instrumentation and heartfelt lyrics. Its two minor hits got little play on the radio and MTV, but the album sold well enough to fund a follow-up. The band rented an abandoned church for fourteen months and spent that time trying to capture specific sounds and piece them together as a whole. The result was *Spirit of Eden*, an acoustic album with a single twenty-minute song on one side and nothing approaching a single on the other. One reviewer wrote that the lyrics "abstractly embrace such thigh-slapping subject matter as moral decline, drug addiction and that perennial party-starter, death. Commercially, it is hard to envisage the album as 'a goer.'"

It wasn't. Critics loved it, but *Spirit of Eden* was a flop. Talk Talk's label, EMI, first sued and then cut ties with the band. Talk Talk did one more album, for a jazz label, before disbanding in 1992. Six years later, Hollis recorded a solo album and then left the music industry for good, opting to focus on being "a good dad."

But his impact persisted . . . not in pop singles but in changed lives.

In 1987, at the end of his freshman year of college, Brad Birzer spotted *The Colour of Spring* at a record store. Taken with the album cover—a wild collection of colored moths—he bought it. Birzer, who was a "rather proud agnostic and skeptic at the time," found the intensity and mysticism of the music utterly compelling. He couldn't make out all the lyrics, and the album had no lyric sheet, but he listened to the album repeatedly for a year, studying and analyzing every aspect of it. And, inspired to understand the sacred, he began to practice the Catholic faith that he had abandoned.

In April 1988, on a visit to London, Birzer found the lyric sheet of *The Colour of Spring* in a London record store. "As I stood reading the T. S. Eliot-esque lyrics—especially as a newly-returned-to-the-faith Roman Catholic—I began to sob," he recalls. "The lyrics were even better and more Christian than I had guessed, and so much of my life—the good, the bad, the misunderstood—came together in that moment. At that point in my life, nothing could have seemed more beautiful or more perfectly timed. Standing there, I felt forgiveness and redemption—toward myself and others. And, I realized that artistry really could make the fallen world a bit better."

While working at a campus radio station his junior year, Birzer received an advanced copy of *The Spirit of Eden*. He and his friend Kevin McCormick "listened to it in complete silence, each of us overwhelmed by its depths." Three years later, the final Talk Talk album "energized me intellectually and spiritually."

Birzer and McCormick went their separate ways after college. Birzer pursued his doctorate and today is a professor and the head of the history department at Hillsdale College in Michigan. McCormick became a classical guitarist, composer, and teacher in Texas. But the music of Mark Hollis has been a key part of their lives for over three decades. "April 5" is one of the tracks on *The Colour of Spring, and* every April fifth the friends listen to the entire album to honor a pact they made in college.

When Hollis died in 2019, Birzer wrote this: "Thank you, Mark David Hollis. You ran the race, and you fought the good fight. Now, it's time to rest your head . . . in the love of He whom you praised again and again in your art."[4]

God is the giver of life. Jesus came that we might have life, and have it abundantly. The closer we get to God, the more we experience that abundant life. In what we see. In what we feel.

And in what we hear.

PRAYER

God, I get so bound up by the details of life that I forget to live. Breathe fresh life into me so I can experience the fullness of life, joy, and peace in You. You are the way, the truth, and the life that I need. Amen.

Questions for Reflection and Application
1. Talk Talk sang that "life's what you make it." How do you feel about that sentiment?
2. What things make you feel alive? What things make you feel close to God? Are they the same things?
3. What tends to suck the life out of you? How do you deal with that? How should you?
4. What did Jesus mean by "life to the full"?
5. In what areas of your life do you settle for just getting by? Why do you settle?
6. What does God want you to do when you are not experiencing abundant life?

Light

Bible Passages

1. **Genesis 1:1–5** – On the first day, God creates light

2. **Psalm 27** – God is your light and salvation

3. **Psalm 43** – God sends light and truth to lead you

4. **Matthew 5:14–16** – You are the light of the world

5. **John 1:1–13** – Jesus is the Word and the light

6. **1 Thessalonians 5:1–11** – We are children of light

7. **1 John 2:7–11** – If you walk in light, then you love your brother

Again Jesus spoke to them, saying, "I am the light of the world. Whoever follows me will not walk in darkness, but will have the light of life."

—*John 8:12*

Plants need light. So do people.

Light from the sun is essential to the process of photosynthesis, whereby plants use the energy from light to convert carbon dioxide and water into carbohydrates, which provide the plants with energy. The process gives off a by-product of oxygen, which animals, and people, need to survive.

Light from the sun is also essential to the emotional well-being of millions of people. Lack of sun exposure during the shorter daylight hours of the late fall and winter signal the brain to create too much of the hormone melatonin, which can lead to a mood disorder called seasonal depression or seasonal affective disorder (SAD). The disorder affects men and women equally, with men's symptoms trending toward irritability, anger, and frustration.

Most sufferers can combat SAD with light therapy, absorbing full-spectrum light from a light box for at least thirty minutes every day. A light box provides 10,000 lux, which is 100 times brighter than usual indoor lighting but five times less bright than a sunny day. When you keep your eyes open, the bright light stimulates cells in your retina that connect to your hypothalamus, the part of your brain that helps control circadian rhythms.[5]

We need light for much more than mood regulation. Without light, we cannot see. Animals such as bats and dolphins can navigate in the dark using echolocation, where the animal emits a sound and determines the location of objects by listening to reflections of that sound. Some blind people also use echolocation.

Most of us, however, stumble in the dark. We do the same thing in our spiritual lives. We need light to find our way.

God's Word, the Bible, provides some of the light we need. It provides a lamp to our feet and a light to our path (see Psalm 119:105). It gives us understanding (see Psalm 119:130). It is "profitable for teaching, for reproof, for correction, and for training in righteousness, that the man of God may be complete, equipped for every good work" (2 Timothy 3:16–17).

But we need more, just as God's chosen people in the Old Testament needed more. They had God's Law. They knew that, if they meditated on it and were careful to follow it, then they would prosper and "have good success" (Joshua 1:8). But the people still walked, and lived, in darkness (see Isaiah 9:2), and that darkness would continue to cover the earth and surround all people (see Isaiah 60:2).

Even the wisest man in the Old Testament needed more. God gave Solomon "wisdom and understanding beyond measure, and breadth of mind like the sand on the seashore" (1 Kings 4:29). People of all nations came to hear the wisdom of Solomon. He spoke 3,000 proverbs and wrote over 1,000 songs. But he strayed from God, and, at the end of his life, Solomon wrote, "I have seen everything that is done under the sun, and behold, all is vanity and a striving after wind" (Ecclesiastes 1:14).

God promised His people that He would send the light that they desperately needed, one that would reveal His glory. That light would come to earth as a child: *For to us a child is born, to us a son is given; and the government shall be upon his shoulder, and his name shall be called Wonderful Counselor, Mighty God, Everlasting Father, Prince of Peace.* (Isaiah 9:6)

That child, of course, was Jesus. The Gospel of John opens with an explanation that Jesus, the Word, was with God in the beginning and is God. "In him was life, and the life was the light of men. The light shines in the darkness, and the darkness has not overcome it" (1:4–5). The "true light, which gives light to everyone" (1:9), came into the world as Jesus. "I am the light of the world," Jesus confirms later in that Gospel. "Whoever follows me will not walk in darkness, but will have the light of life" (8:12).

By following Jesus, we have the light that we need for forgiveness (1 John 1:7) and a full life. And we can share that light with others.

Early in the Sermon on the Mount (see Matthew 5–7), Jesus says that his followers have his light in them. The evidence of that light is not what we say but the good works that we do. When we seek to glorify God in our actions, our light can burn so brightly that others can't help but notice. If they respond by giving us accolades, then we can point them to God, who powers the light within us.

They, in turn, will glorify God, just as we do.

PRAYER

Holy Spirit, use Your light to reveal new truths to me. Help me to spot those people whom God has placed in my path, so that I may reflect Your light to them. Amen.

Questions for Reflection and Application

1. The first time God speaks in the Bible, it is to create light. Why do you think that is?
2. How much does light affect your mood? Do you struggle more when you get less sunlight, such as on overcast days or winter days (or overcast winter days, which you get for three straight months in northeast Ohio)? How do you deal with having less light?
3. In what areas of your life have you preferred to "walk in darkness"? Why?
4. Where do you need more of God's light? What is your plan for getting it?
5. Just as the moon reflects the sun's light, we are to reflect God's light. In what situations is that easy for you? In what situations is that more difficult?

Love

Bible Passages

1. **Psalm 36** – Praise for God's steadfast love

2. **Psalm 136** – His steadfast love endures forever

3. **Lamentations 3:19–27** – God's love is new every morning

4. **Micah 7:18–20** – God's compassionate love

5. **Romans 8:31–39** – Nothing can separate us from God's love

6. **Ephesians 3:14–19** – God's love surpasses understanding

7. **1 John 4:7–21** – We love because God first loved us

. . . you, being rooted and grounded in love, may have strength to comprehend with all the saints what is the breadth and length and height and depth, and to know the love of Christ that surpasses knowledge . . .

—*Ephesians 3:17b–19a*

Jesus and his disciples traveled throughout the region of Galilee. In each village, Jesus taught everyone who would listen and healed everyone who was brought to him with any malady. One day, in the middle of this grueling schedule, Jesus received word that John the Baptist had been executed by Herod. Jesus tried to go off by himself for a time.

But the crowds gave him no time. When they heard that he had withdrawn by himself to a desolate place, they followed him there. By the thousands. So he taught them. He healed their sick. And when evening came and they had nothing to eat, he fed them dinner. Five thousand men, along with women and children, were fed from five loaves of bread and two small fish.

After he dismissed the crowd, Jesus instructed his disciples to cross the Sea of Galilee. A few hours later, he did something that may seem a little out of character: *And in the fourth watch of the night he came to them, walking on the sea. But when the disciples saw him walking on the sea, they were terrified, and said, "It is a ghost!" and they cried out in fear.* (Matthew 14:25–26)

Why did Jesus do that? To show more of his amazing abilities? To prove that he was greater than Moses, who parted the Red Sea? To fulfill Isaiah 43:2? To remind his disciples to trust in him?

Or was there some other reason?

In the famous 1 Corinthians 13 passage (which you must, by law, have read at your wedding), Paul explains that, if you don't have love, then speaking in tongues, prophetic powers, discernment, faith, generosity, sacrifice—everything else—is pointless. True love is patient, kind, humble, selfless, sacrificial, good, true, steadfast, hopeful, and, well, perfect.

It's also impossible, without God. We can't love others—not the way we are commanded to love them—without God's help. That's because "love is from God, and whoever loves has been born of God and knows God. Anyone who does not love does not know God, because God is love" (1 John 4:7–8).

The Bible has been called the story of God's love for us, his people. The Old Testament is a collection of stories that follow the same pattern: God loves us. We turn our backs on Him. He calls us to repent and return. And the cycle repeats. The New Testament starts the story over, this time with God revealing His love for His people by sending His Son. Jesus demonstrated that love in everything he did. Including walking on water.

Before the crowd arrived, Jesus was grappling with the death of John the Baptist. To Jesus, John wasn't a random wilderness preacher. The two were born about six months apart, and their mothers were relatives. John started his ministry first, to prepare the way for Jesus. "I baptize you with water for repentance," said John, "but he who is coming after me is mightier than I, whose sandals I am not worthy to carry" (Matthew 3:11). When Jesus started his own ministry, he asked John to baptize him, even though John objected (see Matthew 3:13–15). Later, when John was in prison, he sent some of his disciples to Jesus to confirm that Jesus was the Messiah, and Jesus sent back a message of confirmation and reassurance (see Matthew 11:2–6).

When John was executed, Jesus needed some time to himself—to mourn John's death and to pray. When Jesus saw that a crowd had gathered, however, he cut short his mourning and ministered to the people. After that, he sent his disciples off on the sea so that he finally could have some time to himself. Once again, his time was cut short, because the boat was caught in a terrible storm, and the disciples needed his help. Right now. In the middle of the night.

So Jesus went to them. Right to them. By walking across the water. He didn't do it to scare them, or to impress them, or to make some point about his divine nature. He did it because they needed him, and walking across the water was the most direct and expedient way to get there.

He did it for the same reason that he had ministered to the crowd hours earlier. He did it because he loved them.

Prophecies pass away. Tongues cease. Knowledge passes away. Love never ends.

PRAYER

God, I'll never grasp how much You love me. Help me to love others, even those who are as tough to love as I am. Amen

Questions for Reflection and Application

1. Why did God choose to love people who turned against Him repeatedly?

2. Of all the ways that God has demonstrated His love for you, which are the most meaningful to you?

3. Do you tend to thank God for His love or take it for granted? How can you thank Him in a meaningful way for His love for you?

4. The New Testament was written primarily in Greek, a language that has four words for love: (1) *eros*, or romantic love; (2) *philia*, or affectionate regard, usually for a close friend; (3) *storge*, or familial love; and (4) *agape*, or unconditional love (God's love). How can you demonstrate *agape* to your wife or girlfriend? To your close friends? To your family members? To people whom you don't know well?

5. In John 15, Jesus says that the ultimate expression of love for someone is laying down your life for that person. For which people would you make the ultimate sacrifice? For which people would you not? Why?

Peace

Bible Passages

1. **1 Chronicles 22:17–19** – God gives peace

2. **Isaiah 9:2–7** – Jesus is the Prince of Peace

3. **Isaiah 26:1–9** – Trusting in God brings you peace

4. **Luke 2:25–35** – Simeon's peace

5. **John 14:25–28** – Jesus leaves peace with his disciples

6. **Philippians 4:4–7** – God's peace surpasses understanding

7. **Colossians 3:12–17** – Let peace rule in your heart

And the peace of God, which surpasses all understanding, will guard your hearts and your minds in Christ Jesus.

—Philippians 4:7

More than three decades before Peter Jackson adapted J. R. R. Tolkein's *The Lord of the Rings* trilogy in three epic films, Sergei Bondarchuk adapted Leo Tolstoy's novel *War and Peace* as a single epic movie. That movie was so long—over seven hours—that it originally was released in four parts over three years. It is still considered the most ambitious film ever made.

When most of us think of peace, we think of it in relation to war, as in Tolstoy's novel or Bondarchuk's film. Peace is the opposite of war, or the absence of conflict. When we read in the Bible that God will bless His people with peace (see Psalm 29:11), that the Messiah is to be the Prince of Peace (see Isaiah 9:6), and that peace is part of the fruit of the Spirit (see Galatians 5:22), we may think that God blesses His people with the absence of conflict, that Jesus reigns over a kingdom where there is no war, and that the Holy Spirit empowers us to end conflict.

But there's a war raging. There has been since the dawn of time. It started when Satan rebelled against God and fell from heaven "like lightning" (Luke 10:18). Since then, the forces of evil have been at war with the forces of good. That's why one of the prominent names for God in the Old Testament is *Yahweh Sabaoth*: the Lord of hosts or, more literally, the God of angel armies. The war will continue until the end of time, when God wins.

In a universe at war, what kind of peace does God offer?

Shortly after Jesus was born, his parents took him to the temple in Jerusalem to present him to God. There, they met a righteous man named Simeon. The Holy Spirit had told Simeon that he would see the Messiah, the Christ, before he died. Once he saw Jesus, Simeon took the baby in his arms, praised God, and said that he could die in peace, because he had seen God's salvation.

Another biblical character who died in peace was Josiah. He became the king of Judah when he was just eight and, unlike his predecessors, he followed God faithfully. He purged Judah of idols and the priests of false gods. He restored the temple, and the high priest discovered the Book of the Law, or Torah, there. When Josiah heard it read, he tore his clothes and commanded the high priest to ask God what to do. God responded that, although He would bring disaster upon Judah, Josiah would not see it, because his heart was penitent and had humbled himself before God. Josiah, God said, would die in peace.

Josiah proceeded to enact reforms and restore the celebration of the Passover. Thirteen years later, Josiah went out to fight against the king of Egypt. While Josiah was approaching the battlefield in his chariot, archers shot him, badly wounding him. His servants took him back to Jerusalem, where he died. He was thirty-nine.

Um, wait a minute. Let me read 2 Chronicles 35 again.

Yep. That's what it says.

How is being shot with a bunch of arrows dying in peace?

In the Old Testament, the word translated as "peace" is the Hebrew word *shalom*. It appears 237 times, including Isaiah 9:6: *For to us a child is born, to us a son is given; and the government shall be upon his shoulder, and his name shall be called Wonderful Counselor, Mighty God, Everlasting Father, Prince of Peace.*

New Testament writers used the Greek word *eiréné* in place of *shalom*. It appears ninety-two times, including Philippians 4:7: *And the peace of God, which surpasses all understanding, will guard your hearts and your minds in Christ Jesus.*

Shalom means not just peace but also completeness, soundness, and welfare. Similarly, *eiréné* means not just peace but also oneness, quietness, and rest.

Simeon died as an old man, presumably of natural causes, but that's not why he died in peace. Simeon had *eiréné* because God had fulfilled the promise of allowing Simeon to see the one who would bring salvation for all people, Jews and Gentiles alike. Josiah died as a young man, not from natural causes but probably from loss of blood. He had *shalom*, however, because he had followed God faithfully and led the people of Judah to do the same.

God is a God of *shalom* and *eiréné*. His peace—completeness, oneness, rest—is beyond our understanding. But He gives it to us anyway.

PRAYER

God, only you can give me true peace, including completeness, soundness, oneness, quietness, and rest. Remind me to cast my cares on You and rely on You, not myself, for peace. Amen.

Questions for Reflection and Application

1. Rank the aspects of *shalom* and *eiréné*—peace, completeness, soundness, oneness, quietness, and rest—from most important to least important for you. How would your rankings have been different ten years ago? How will they be different ten years from now?

2. What does Prince of Peace mean to you? What images does it bring to mind?

3. What would it mean for you to be at peace?

4. What evidence have you seen that there is a war raging in the spiritual realm?

5. We often say that we want peace and quiet, where quiet is the absence of noise. These days, noise doesn't have to be audible; we can get "noise" in our lives from work, from home, from media and social media, and from many other places. What are the primary sources of "noise" in your life? How can you get the peace and quiet you seek?

Power

Bible Passages

1. **Exodus 6:1–8** – God sends Moses to show His power

2. **Psalm 24** – The LORD of Hosts is the King of glory

3. **Psalm 68** – David praises God's power

4. **Luke 1:46–55** – Mary praises her mighty God

5. **Ephesians 3:20–21** – God can do anything for us

6. **Colossians 1:15–20** – The full power of God dwells in Jesus

7. **Revelation 4** – God is worthy of all glory, honor, and power

Now to him who is able to do far more abundantly than all that we ask or think, according to the power at work within us, to him be glory in the church and in Christ Jesus throughout all generations, forever and ever. Amen.

—Ephesians 3:20–21

M ost of the kids in the youth group that I helped lead didn't ask tough questions. But Kevin did. He seemed to specialize in them.

One evening, he hit me with this: "Jesus was God, right? So he could do anything. When he was up on the cross, he had the power to come down from there, right?"

"Right," I said.

"Why didn't he?"

I don't remember my answer. I hope that I mentioned the resurrection.

For two centuries, writes Catholic bishop Robert Barron, various "thinkers" and even prominent theologians have tried to "domesticate" the resurrection. Some have argued that it is simply a symbol or a metaphor. Others have reduced it to a myth or an archetype, patterned after the many stories of dying and rising gods in the mythologies of the world.

But mythic narratives are situated "once upon a time," with no historical specificity. New Testament narratives, on the other hand, provide all kinds of details about the life, death, and resurrection of Jesus, including names of people who saw him alive after that first Easter Sunday. A symbolic event would not have generated the sheer excitement evident in those narratives and in the preaching of the first Christians. And how many followers of Jesus would have sacrificed everything, including their lives, if Jesus had not risen from the dead?[6]

In 1 Corinthians 15:17–19, Paul pins everything on the resurrection:

If Christ has not been raised, your faith is futile and you are still in your sins. Then those also who have fallen asleep in Christ have perished. If in Christ we have hope in this life only, we are of all people most to be pitied.

Then he opens the next paragraph by asserting that God did, indeed, raise Jesus from the dead. How did God do it? As Paul explains in Ephesians 1, the resurrection was a demonstration of God's immeasurable power, which He "worked in Christ when he raised him from the dead and seated him at his right hand in the heavenly places, far above all rule and authority and power and dominion, and above every name that is named, not only in this age but also in the one to come" (vv. 20–21).

That same power is even in the name of Jesus. An early Christian hymn, recorded by Paul in Philippians 2, explains that God gave Jesus "the name that is above every name, so that at the name of Jesus every knee should bow, in heaven and on earth and under the earth, and every tongue confess that Jesus Christ is Lord, to the glory of God the Father" (vv. 9–11).

Missionary E. P. Scott witnessed that power. While in a major city in India, Scott saw a man from a savage mountain tribe that had never heard the gospel. Over the objections of senior missionaries, Scott decided to witness to the tribe. When he reached the mountains, near the tribe's village, he suddenly found himself surrounded by tribesmen, all pointing their spears at his heart. Expecting to die at any moment, Scott took out his violin, said a prayer quietly, closed his eyes, and began to play and sing "All Hail the Power of Jesus' Name." He made it through the first verse. Then the second.

As he sang the third verse, Scott opened his eyes. The spears had dropped, and some of the warriors had tears in their eyes. He spent the next thirty months with the tribe, telling them about Jesus and his love for them. When poor health forced Scott to leave the tribe, the tribespeople walked forty miles with him to a point where he could obtain other transportation.[7]

These and other stories make it clear that God is powerful. So why didn't God use that power to prevent two world wars? Or the Holocaust? Or the 9/11 attacks? Why doesn't God use His power to solve all the world's problems today? Or yours?

Perhaps the answer lies in 2 Corinthians 12. Paul had a "thorn," or "a messenger of Satan" to harass him. He pleaded that God would remove the thorn, but God replied, "My grace is sufficient for you, for my power is made perfect in weakness" (v. 9). By being content with his weaknesses—and insults, hardships, persecutions, and calamities—Paul found that the power of Christ rested upon him all the more. When he was weak, he was strong.

PRAYER

Lord God, Your power holds the universe in place, slays armies, and performs miracles. Forgive me when my mind tries to limit what You can do. Nothing is too great for You. I thank You that You are in control. Amen.

Questions for Reflection and Application

1. What is your answer to Kevin's question?
2. Are you convinced, beyond a shadow of a doubt, that the resurrection of Jesus happened? If not, then what would it take to convince you? If so, then could you offer a compelling case to someone who doesn't believe that it happened?
3. What is your immediate reaction when you hear an amazing story of God's power? Why do you react that way?
4. What evidence of God's power have you witnessed in the past year?
5. What are some areas of your life where God did not use His power as you wish He had? Why didn't God do it? What happened as a result?
6. Are you like Paul, content with your weaknesses, because they demonstrate your reliance on God's power? Why or why not?

Righteousness

Bible Passages

1. **Genesis 15:1–6** – Abram's faith is counted as righteousness

2. **Psalm 7** – God is a righteous judge

3. **Psalm 112** – The righteous will never be moved

4. **Isaiah 11** – A prophecy of the righteous reign of Jesus

5. **Romans 3:21–31** – We attain righteousness through faith

6. **2 Corinthians 5** – In Christ we become righteous

7. **Philippians 3:2–11** – Righteousness through faith in Christ

For his sake I have suffered the loss of all things and count them as rubbish, in order that I may gain Christ and be found in him, not having a righteousness of my own that comes from the law, but that which comes through faith in Christ, the righteousness from God that depends on faith . . .

—Philippians 3:8b–9

He had no experience, so he winged it. He had no credentials, so he invented some. He forged documents. He bribed officials.

All to save the lives of 669 children he'd never met. Children who, for fifty years, had no idea who he was or what he had done.

In 1938, violence against Jews was escalating in Germany. Once the Munich Agreement was signed, Nazi troops marched unopposed into the Sudetenland, the German-speaking region of Czechoslovakia. Sensing that war was coming, Czech Jews began trying to get their children out of the country.

In London, a successful twenty-nine-year-old stockbroker named Nicholas Winton heard news reports of "German persecution" in Czechoslovakia and wanted to help. Early in 1939 he used a two-week vacation to go to Prague. There he saw camps where 150,000 refugees, including children, faced brutal conditions.

From his hotel room, Winton set up a small organization to get as many children as possible out of the country. Once Czech Jews found out, several hundred came to him, providing him with information on their children in the hopes that he might save them.

Once back in London, he had to convince British authorities to take him seriously. So, he took stationary from an established refugee organization, added "Children's Section", and made himself chairman. From a tiny office in central London, Winton's mother and a team of volunteers worked all day, and Winton worked nights after his day job as a stockbroker.

The US government refused to help. The British government agreed to accept children into the country only if Winton found families to take them. He found willing families, but British authorities were slow in issuing travel documents, so Winton started having them forged. He also bribed people.

The first twenty children left Prague on March 14, 1939. Violence against Jews spread, but the Nazis allowed Winton's trains to travel, in keeping with their policy to "cleanse" Europe of Jews. In six months, seven trains carried 669 children through the heart of Germany to Holland, where they took a ferry to the English coast. From there, they caught a train to London.

An eighth train, carrying 250 more, was scheduled to leave Prague on September 1. But war was declared that day, and the train never left. 77,300 Czech Jews later were eliminated as part of the "Final Solution."

Once Winton could no longer help Czech children, he shut down the "Children's Section." During the war he volunteered for a Red Cross ambulance unit, then trained pilots for the Royal Air Force. He got married, raised a family, and lived as an ordinary person, telling virtually no one what he had done. "I didn't really keep it secret," he said in 2014. "I just didn't talk about it."

In 1988, the BBC learned about Winton's story and began to publicize what he had done. Fifteen years later, Winton was knighted. He became a national hero in the Czech Republic. He didn't like the adulation. "I'm not interested in the past," he said. He preferred to concentrate on the present and the future. For the last fifty years of his life, Winton helped mentally handicapped people and built homes for the elderly.

Throughout his life, he tried to do the right thing. And succeeded.

In the Bible, the words for "righteous" also mean "just." When we say that God is righteous or just, we are saying that He always does what is right, or what should be done. God's actions always are right and fair. He sets the standard for righteousness.

For us, righteousness is a measurement of how closely we conform to that standard. When we forsake God, we find it impossible to be righteous (see Psalm 14). The more closely we follow God, the more we can be righteous. Jesus promised that those who hunger and thirst for righteousness will be satisfied (see Matthew 5:6). How? The sinless Jesus became a sin offering for us, and through Jesus we may become the righteousness of God (see 2 Corinthians 5:21).

Winton died in 2015 at the age of 106. The 669 children he saved got married and had children of their own. Their children did the same, as did their grandchildren. Today, over 15,000 people owe their lives to a humble man who saw a need—a desperate need—and did whatever was necessary to meet that need.[8]

A righteous man.

PRAYER
Lord God, let Your righteousness infuse and permeate my life. Amen.

Questions for Reflection and Application
1. What actions of God reveal His righteousness?
2. If God is righteous, then why does He allow some unrighteous and even wicked people to prosper?
3. How much do you hunger and thirst for righteousness? For what things do you hunger and thirst more?
4. In whom have you seen glimpses of righteousness in your world? How did this person's example affect you? Others?
5. Sanctification is a growth process through which you become more righteous and more holy. In what regular practices do you engage to become more righteous? What is one additional practice that you could adopt to grow in sanctification?
6. Do you have to be pious, or faithfully devoted to religion, to be righteous? Why or why not?

Salvation

Bible Passages

1. **Matthew 1:18–25** – "Jesus" means "God saves"

2. **Luke 1:67–79** – Zechariah's prophecy: salvation through forgiveness

3. **Luke 23:39–43** – One criminal on a cross is saved

4. **Romans 10:5–13** – Paul explains the way of salvation

5. **Ephesians 2:1–10** – We are saved by grace through faith

6. **Titus 3:3–7** – God showed us mercy by saving us

7. **1 Peter 1:3–9** – We are born again to a living hope

For what will it profit a man if he gains the whole world and forfeits his soul? Or what shall a man give in return for his soul?

—*Matthew 16:26*

I n the days of Jesus, rich men were considered blessed by God. But they were the bad guys in a few of Jesus's parables. In the parable of the rich fool (see Luke 12:16–21), a man who "lays up treasure for himself and is not rich toward God" has a bumper crop that will supply his needs for a long time. He plans to "eat, drink, be merry" for many years, but he dies before he can enjoy any of it. In the parable of the rich man and Lazarus (see Luke 16:19–31), a rich man who "was clothed in purple and fine linen and who feasted sumptuously every day" dies, as does a poor man named Lazarus, whom the rich man ignored. Lazarus ends up in heaven; the rich man ends up in torment in Hades.

As *A Christmas Carol* opens, the bad guy is another rich man: Ebenezer Scrooge. The ghost of Scrooge's former partner, Jacob Marley, is burdened with a heavy chain that he forged in life— link after link of missed opportunities to help others. "Mankind was my business," he bellows to Scrooge. "The common welfare was my business; charity, mercy, forbearance, and benevolence, were, all, my business." And Scrooge's chain is even heavier. To escape Marley's fate, Scrooge will have to heed three spirits that will visit him that night, Christmas Eve.

When the first spirit shows him past Christmases, Scrooge sees the only woman who ever loved him. They were engaged to be married, until Scrooge's fear of poverty caused him to fall in love with another. "All your other hopes have merged into the hope of being beyond the chance of its sordid reproach," she told him. "I have seen your nobler aspirations fall off one by one, until the master-passion, Gain, engrosses you." The pair no longer had a chance at happiness, so they ended their engagement. And she went on to a life of joy with another man.

On a tour of present-day Christmases with the second spirit, Scrooge sees his only living relative, a nephew, the child of Scrooge's dead sister. Every year, the nephew invites Scrooge over for Christmas, and every year Scrooge refuses. "Who suffers by his ill whims?" the nephew asks his guests. "Himself, always. Here, he takes it into his head to dislike us, and he won't come and dine with us." The consequence? Scrooge loses pleasant moments with pleasant people.

By the time the Ghost of Christmas Future arrives, Scrooge claims to be ready to "live to be another man" from what he was. But first, he must endure seeing a host of people who seem happy that an unidentified man has died. When Scrooge asks to see "some tenderness connected with a death," the spirit shows him the family of Scrooge's worker Bob Crachit, struggling to cope with the death of their young son, Tiny Tim. Finally, the spirit confirms that the previously unidentified dead man is Scrooge.

"I am not the man I was," pleads Scrooge. "I will not be the man I must have been but for this intercourse. Why show me this, if I am past all hope?" Vowing to change his life, Scrooge awakens.

It is Christmas Day. And Scrooge is a new man.

Can someone who led a life of sin go to heaven by virtue of accepting Jesus late in life, even on his deathbed? The story of the thief on the cross (see Luke 23:39–43) offers clear support for this. So does the parable of the workers in the vineyard (see Matthew 20:1–16), where all the day laborers are paid the same wage, regardless of when they started working that day.

Of course, salvation is not something you earn. It's a gift, one that none of us deserves (see Romans 3:23–24) but which is offered freely to all who agree to repent and follow Jesus with their whole heart. Some people procrastinate on the repenting and following bit. The cost of that is pretty high, they figure, and they don't want to pay it right now. They'll get to it later.

Sure, there's a cost. But there's an even bigger benefit, one that you get immediately. The assurance of salvation brings you joy. That joy enables you to do what is impossible without salvation—enjoy, and even rejoice in, whatever life sends your way.

Marley didn't understand that until it was too late. Scrooge found out just in time.

Scrooge was better than his word. He did it all, and infinitely more; and to Tiny Tim, who did NOT die, he was a second father. He became as good a friend, as good a master, and as good a man, as the good old city knew...and it was always said of him, that he knew how to keep Christmas well, if any man alive possessed the knowledge. May that be truly said of us, and all of us![9]

PRAYER
Jesus, thank you for providing salvation to a man like me. Amen.

Questions for Reflection and Application
1. Most mentions of salvation in the Old Testament refer to God saving His people from physical threats, including those posed by enemies and evildoers. From what physical threats do you need help from God? Do you know others who need God's salvation from similar threats?
2. Most mentions of salvation in the New Testament refer to God saving His people from hell, or eternal separation from God. How is this similar to the Old Testament notion of salvation? How is it different?
3. Why was it necessary for Jesus to die on the cross?
4. How confident are you that you are saved (as described in the New Testament)? If you are not 100 percent confident, then what doubts do you have? How can you get those doubts addressed?
5. How does the gift of salvation impact your life here on earth? How are you demonstrating that impact?

Truth

Bible Passages

1. **Psalm 25:1–10** – God leads us in truth

2. **Psalm 119:152–160** – God's Word offers truth

3. **John 8:31–38** – The truth will set you free

4. **John 14:1–7** – Jesus is the way, the truth, and the life

5. **Romans 1:18–25** – Unrighteous people exchange the truth of God for lies

6. **Ephesians 1:11–14** – Hear the word of truth, believe, and be saved

7. **2 John 1–6** – Walk in truth and love

"If you abide in my word, you are truly my disciples, and you will know the truth, and the truth will set you free."

—*John 8:31b–32*

P ontius Pilate is a name that lives in infamy. Identified as the Roman governor of Judea in Luke 3:1, Pilate is mentioned in all four Gospels—Matthew 27:24-26, Mark 15:15, Luke 23:24-25, and John 19:15-16—as the person who gave the official order for Jesus to be crucified. The Apostles' Creed says that Jesus "suffered under Pontius Pilate," and the Nicene Creed says that Jesus was "crucified under Pontius Pilate."

The accounts of Jesus before Pilate—with the Jewish leaders and crowd trying to persuade Pilate to sentence Jesus to death— are nearly identical in the Gospels of Matthew and Mark. The only significant difference is a single verse (shown in boldface type):

Pilate said to them, "Whom do you want me to release for you: Barabbas, or Jesus who is called Christ?" For he knew that it was out of envy that they had delivered him up. **Besides, while he was sitting on the judgment seat, his wife sent word to him, "Have nothing to do with that righteous man, for I have suffered much because of him today in a dream."** *Now the chief priests and the elders persuaded the crowd to ask for Barabbas and destroy Jesus.* (Matthew 27:17–20)

Pilate's wife is not named. She does not appear anywhere else in the Bible. She lived during a time when the testimony of women was not considered credible. And her warning to her husband did nothing to change the outcome. So why is the verse there? It's a tip-off that Pilate's wife—and Pilate himself—were forever changed by the events of that day.

When you read the four Gospel accounts of Pilate and Jesus, you realize that the Bible not only has intimate details of a private conversation but also tells us how Pilate *felt* about it. Pilate was "amazed" at how Jesus responded to his questions. Pilate wanted to release Jesus. Pilate knew that Jewish religious leaders were envious of Jesus. How can such private information be there? There are four possibilities:

1. **God revealed the details to the Gospel writers.** If that is the case, then why do different Gospels have different details? And why did God provide these details?

2. **Jesus told the disciples, who passed along the information.** Given that Jesus had a very limited time with his disciples before he ascended, it seems unlikely that he would have spent that time discussing Pilate.

3. **Another eyewitness told the Gospel writers.** What eyewitness observed a private conversation in Pilate's headquarters? Why would that eyewitness report his observations to the Gospel writers a few decades later? And how would he know what Pilate was thinking or feeling?

4. **Pilate's wife was the reporter.** This is the most likely explanation. She could have known the intimate details because he told her after a dreadful day in which he sent an innocent man to his death. And she would have remembered every detail because of her dream and her warning.

But why would she have told any of the followers of Jesus? And why would they have listened and recorded what she said?

Because she was one of them.

According to certain segments of the Orthodox Christian Church, Pilate's wife, who sometimes is given the name Procula Claudia, converted to Christianity after the resurrection and was executed as a Christian. The second-century Christian scholar and theologian Origen suggested that God sent Pilate's wife the dream so that she might come to know Christ. Other theologians have supported this view.

And the news gets even better. In Hurghada, Egypt, there is an icon of both Procula Claudia and Pontius Pilate. Coptic Christians venerate *both* as saints. In other words, they believe that the man who sentenced Jesus to death became a follower of Jesus and likely was executed for his faith.[10]

Perhaps one critical exchange with Jesus made all the difference:

Then Pilate said to him, "So you are a king?" Jesus answered, "You say that I am a king. For this purpose I was born and for this purpose I have come into the world—to bear witness to the truth. Everyone who is of the truth listens to my voice." Pilate said to him, "What is truth?" (John 18:37–38)

Ultimately, Pilate and his wife, like other followers of Jesus, learned the truth. And the truth set them free.

PRAYER

God, Your Word is truth, and the truth sets us free. I thank you for the Bible and marvel that every verse in it is there to enlighten, strengthen, and encourage me. Amen.

Questions for Reflection and Application

1. When you are trying to determine if something is true, what is your methodology? Why do you take that approach?

2. In John 18, Pilate asks Jesus, "What is truth?" In the next chapter, it appears that Pilate has learned the answer and tries everything he can do to set Jesus free. Describe a situation where you knew the right thing to do and didn't do it. Why did you do the wrong thing?

3. In the description of the armor of God (see Ephesians 6:10–20), why is truth a belt?

4. Why does John tell us to walk in truth and love? How do people sometimes walk in love without truth? Truth without love?

5. How does the truth set you free?

Will

Bible Passages

1. **Genesis 1:26–30** – God's plan for mankind

2. **2 Samuel 22:26–40** – God's way is perfect

3. **Job 42:1–6** – No purpose of God can be thwarted

4. **Jeremiah 29:4–13** – God's plan for Israelite exiles

5. **Mark 3:31–35** – Whoever does God's will is Christ's brother

6. **Romans 11:33–12:2** – Knowing and discerning God's will

7. **1 Timothy 2:1–4** – God wants all people to be saved

"Your kingdom come, your will be done, on earth as it is in heaven."

—*Matthew 6:10*

God has a plan for your life. Everything that happens is part of God's plan. When God closes a door, He opens a window.

These are among the most hated Christian clichés not only because they present a simplistic view of the will of God but also because they usually are uttered to someone who is going through a rough time. And they don't help.

Understanding God's will is important, whatever your situation. The model that Jesus gave us for how to pray—the Lord's Prayer—includes only six requests: (1) your kingdom come, (2) your will be done, (3) give us our daily bread, (4) forgive us (as we forgive), (5) lead us not into temptation, and (6) deliver us from evil. What is God's will, which we pray is done on earth as it is in heaven?

At a high level, God's will is that each of us will love, follow, and serve God. The third chapter of 2 Peter gives us a glimpse into God's heart here. After describing in vivid detail what will happen to ungodly people on the day of judgment, Peter[11] writes that "with the Lord one day is as a thousand years, and a thousand years as one day. The Lord is not slow to fulfill his promise as some count slowness, but is patient toward you, not wishing that any should perish, but that all should reach repentance" (vv. 8–9). In the Gospel of John, Jesus explains that God's will is "that everyone who looks on the Son and believes in him should have eternal life, and I will raise him up on the last day" (6:40).

The problem is that following Jesus is not always easy. After foretelling his death, Jesus said, "If anyone would come after me, let him deny himself and take up his cross daily and follow me" (Luke 9:23). When a rich man who had kept all the commandments asked Jesus how to attain eternal life, Jesus told him to sell everything he had and give it to the poor (see Mark 10:17–22). After explaining that he was sent to do God's will, Jesus delivered a message so troubling that "many of his disciples turned back and no longer walked with him" (John 6:66). So, Jesus asked his twelve closest followers if they were going to leave, too. Peter responded, "Lord, to whom shall we go? You have the words of eternal life" (John 6:68).

God's ultimate plan for you puts you on a course for eternity in heaven. But what is God's will for your life on earth? Does God have a plan for that?

Christians often cite Jeremiah 29:11: "For I know the plans I have for you, declares the Lord, plans for welfare and not for evil, to give you a future and a hope." Sounds great, until you read the rest of the chapter. Jeremiah delivered the message to people who were taken forcibly from Jerusalem to Babylon. They were to make their homes there, have families there, and seek its welfare. After seventy years, when all of them had died there, their children and grandchildren would go back to Jerusalem. The future and hope that God promised was for their descendants.

So how do you know what God's will, and plan, is for you? If Jesus were with us in the flesh, then you could ask him directly and get an answer. That's what a man with leprosy did, in Matthew 8. He knelt before Jesus and said, "Lord, if you will, you can make me clean." Jesus responded immediately, with both words and actions. "I will," he said, as he did the unthinkable and touched the man with the dreaded and highly contagious disease. Then Jesus said, "Be clean!" And instantly the man was cleansed.

Of course, Jesus is not here with us physically. We can pray to him—and the Father, and the Holy Spirit—but we may not get an instant, definitive response. Here is what Paul recommends:

I appeal to you therefore, brothers, by the mercies of God, to present your bodies as a living sacrifice, holy and acceptable to God, which is your spiritual worship. Do not be conformed to this world, but be transformed by the renewal of your mind, that by testing you may discern what is the will of God, what is good and acceptable and perfect. (Romans 12:1–2)

Whatever God's plan is for you, it's the perfect plan. It may not seem that way sometimes, but that's because, as Paul wrote, we see things as dim reflections in a mirror, and we know things only in part. One day we'll see Jesus face to face, and we'll know everything as he does—fully (see 1 Corinthians 13:12). For now, we need to heed Paul's command in 1 Thessalonians 5:16-18: "Rejoice always, pray without ceasing, give thanks in all circumstances; for this is the will of God in Christ Jesus for you."

PRAYER

Your will be done, Father, even when I don't see it or understand it. I give You control. Use me for Your will. Amen.

Questions for Reflection and Application

1. What is God's will for man?
2. What evidence have you seen that God has a plan for your life?
3. Romans 8:28 says that God works all things together for good for those who love Him and who are called according to His purpose. For what has God called you? How are you pursuing that purpose or those purposes?
4. How is God's plan for you similar to His plans for other Christ followers? How is it different?
5. The Lord's Prayer instructs us to pray for God's will and for our daily bread. Does "daily bread" include all our needs? If not, then how and when do we pray for those? What about the needs of others? What other Bible passages can you cite concerning praying for our needs and the needs of others?

God in the Day-to-Day

Do you ever get frustrated that, even though you are a Christian, you can't seem to stop acting like a jerk? Like someone you wouldn't want to be around? Like the worst possible version of yourself?

I know I do. I feel like the guy described in Romans 7:

I do not understand my own actions. For I do not do what I want, but I do the very thing I hate. . . . I have the desire to do what is right, but not the ability to carry it out. For I do not do the good I want, but the evil I do not want is what I keep on doing. Now if I do what I do not want, it is no longer I who do it, but sin that dwells within me.

So I find it to be a law that when I want to do right, evil lies close at hand. For I delight in the law of God, in my inner being, but I see in my members another law waging war against the law of my mind and making me captive to the law of sin that dwells in my members. Wretched man that I am!

That guy, of course, was the apostle Paul. If he describes himself as a wretched man, then what am I? What is a habitual screw-up like me supposed to do?

Fortunately, Paul offers the answer: I go to Jesus. Every day.

Jesus offers me—and you—more than forgiveness. He offers us deliverance, and transformation, from our bodies of death.

In this thirteen-week series, you'll focus on God in your day-to-day life. At your workplace. With your wife or girlfriend. With your family and friends. You'll explore how to battle the forces of evil that plague you on a daily basis and deal with your weaknesses, such as anger, fear, and anxiety. You'll dig into how you can communicate more with God and rely more fully on Him, becoming a more obedient follower, even when you go through deserts where God seems unresponsive.

Daily life doesn't have to be a daily grind. Let Jesus lift you out of your rut.

Anger

Bible Passages

1. **Genesis 49:5–7** – Jacob calls out the anger in his sons
2. **Exodus 32** – God and Moses both get angry
3. **Psalm 4:3–5** – Be angry and do not sin
4. **Mark 11:15–19** – Angry, Jesus cleanses the temple
5. **Galatians 5:15–25** – Anger and sins vs. fruits of the Spirit
6. **Colossians 3:5–11** – Put to death what is earthly, including anger
7. **James 1:19–21** – Anger does not produce righteousness

Be angry and do not sin; do not let the sun go down on your anger, and give no opportunity to the devil.

—*Ephesians 4:26–27*

"I'm sorry I said those things," said Thor to Hulk. "You're not the stupid Avenger. Nobody calls you the stupid Avenger."

"It's okay."

"You just can't go around throwing shields at people. Could've killed me."

"I know. I'm sorry. I just get so angry all the time. Hulk always, always angry."

"We're the same, you and I. Just a couple of hotheaded fools."[12]

Unlike Thor and Hulk, Solomon didn't have anger issues. But he had issues with anger. In Proverbs, he frequently mentions the downsides of being angry. Here are some examples:

- Whoever is slow to anger has great understanding, but he who has a hasty temper exalts folly (14:29).
- Make no friendship with a man given to anger, nor go with a wrathful man (22:24).
- A man of wrath stirs up strife, and one given to anger causes much transgression (29:22).

In his Sermon on the Mount, Jesus implied that anger could be as bad as murder: "You have heard that it was said to those of old, 'You shall not murder; and whoever murders will be liable to judgment.' But I say to you that everyone who is angry with his brother will be liable to judgment" (Matthew 5:21–22a).

In the Bible, God is described as gracious and merciful, slow to anger, and abounding in steadfast love. God may be slow to anger, but He does get angry. The Old Testament records God getting angry with three friends of Job, the people of Israel, Moses and Miriam, the people of Israel, a guy named Uzzah (who touched the Ark of the Covenant), the people of Israel, King

Ahaz and other wicked kings, and the people of Israel, many more times. And Jesus got angry. For example, when he was in a synagogue one Sabbath day, Jesus got angry with some Pharisees who opposed him healing a man because that meant Jesus was doing "work" on the Sabbath, which was against the law (see Mark 3:1–6).

When is anger justified? When is it sinful?

Anger is an emotion, a reaction to something that threatens you or someone you love. Anger has some positive attributes, according to psychologist Stephen Diamond. For example, anger can bestow strength and tenacity in the face of adversity. Without the capacity for anger, we would be unable to defend ourselves and our loved ones, to fight for freedom and other things we value. "We would be unable to face down evil, leaving us even more vulnerable to it."

The problem is not the emotion, Diamond continues, but the actions that it may trigger. Unchecked or misdirected anger can lead to dangerous and destructive behavior. Unfortunately, society often lumps together all expressions of anger and paints them in negative terms. As a result, people feel shame about the emotion of anger and try to repress feeling angry rather than expressing anger in a constructive way.[13]

When you feel angry, you should make sure your anger is justified. When Jesus said "angry" in Matthew 5, the implication was "angry without cause." Even if you have cause for being angry, you should strive to express that anger in a way that leads to reconciliation with the one who is offending you. Otherwise, you may alienate someone close to you, as Paul did.

After his conversion on the road to Damascus, Paul came to Jerusalem to be with the disciples of Jesus, but they were afraid of him. A virtual stranger, Barnabas, vouched for Paul and reassured the disciples that Paul could be trusted. Years later, when Barnabas needed help in Antioch, he went to Tarsus and got Paul, who had been on his own there. After successful work in Antioch, the two friends went on a long missionary journey.

As they prepared for a second such journey, Barnabas suggested that they take his relative Mark, who had deserted them on the first journey. Paul disagreed so strongly that he parted ways with Barnabas. The two never saw each other again.

A decade later, Paul wrote advice that may have been shaped by that experience: "Be angry and do not sin; do not let the sun go down on your anger, and give no opportunity to the devil" (Ephesians 4:26–27).

PRAYER

God, help me to control myself when my anger wants to control me. Remind me to check my motives and my pride, so that I can work through justified anger in constructive ways and stop my selfish anger before I do something stupid. Amen.

Questions for Reflection and Application

1. Look at some of the mentions of God's anger in the Old Testament. What made God angry? How did God express His anger?
2. God's anger is always justified. What percentage of your anger is justified? What are the causes for your justified anger?
3. What situations or events tend to spark your unjustified anger? How can you avoid anger that is unjustified?
4. What have been the consequences, positive and negative, of your anger?
5. What techniques, such as "counting to ten," have you tried to avoid angry outbursts? How well have they worked?
6. How would your heavenly Counselor, the Holy Spirit, advise you on your anger? What steps can you take in the next few months to be angry without sinning?

Conflict

Bible Passages

1. **Genesis 13:1–12** – Abram makes peace with Lot

2. **Psalm 34:4–14** – A righteous man pursues peace

3. **Matthew 5:23–26** – When you sin, go and reconcile

4. **Matthew 18:15–20** – When your brother sins, try to reconcile

5. **Romans 12:14–21** – Live peaceably with all

6. **Ephesians 4:1–7** – Live in peace with other believers

7. **1 Thessalonians 2:1–8** – Share the gospel boldly, even during conflict

"Blessed are the peacemakers, for they shall be called sons of God."

—*Matthew 5:9*

Paden has mastered the art of avoiding conflict. Oh, sure, he'll defend himself. And he'll confront someone who steals from him. But if your illegal or even evil actions don't affect Paden directly, then he'll tend to look the other way.

After he's left for dead on the range, Paden picks up a few new friends: Emmett, who saves Paden's life and then springs him from jail; Emmett's brother Jake, who is sprung from the same jail cell as Paden; and Mal, who helps the trio escape a posse. When the four reach Silverado, they go their separate ways. Paden takes a job co-managing the town saloon, which is owned by the town sheriff, Cobb, with whom Paden used to ride.

Cobb's sweet deal in Silverado has been arranged by Ethan McKendrick, who runs the town and runs off, or kills, anyone who gets in his way. When Emmett and Jake rebuff an attempt by McKendrick's men to terrorize some recent settlers, McKendrick informs Cobb that Emmett, Jake, and Mal have to go. Cobb passes the word along to Paden, after giving Paden a big bonus.

"The fellows you came to town with are causing some trouble. It's going to take a little straightening out. I have responsibilities. I want you to understand. It has nothing to do with us."

"What is it you want from me?" asks Paden.

"Nothing. Do nothing. Don't get between us."

"I'm a great believer in doing nothing," says Paden.

Many of us are like Paden. If someone's sinful actions don't harm us, then we do nothing. We avoid conflict, and even confrontation that may lead to conflict. Better to keep the peace, we argue.

Peacekeepers are not listed among the blessed in the Beatitudes of Matthew 5. Peace*makers* are. Making peace often involves conflict. That's because we live in a world at war, and our enemy "prowls around like a roaring lion, seeking someone to devour" (1 Peter 5:8). The devil landed the first blow in the garden, as Paul explains in Romans 5:12: "Therefore, just as sin came into the world through one man, and death through sin, and so death spread to all men because all sinned." Our sin separated us from God, and the Law did not repair the rift. We stood condemned, and we couldn't break free from the enemy's grip. We needed a savior, one who would battle the devil head on.

That savior, of course, was Jesus. He defeated the devil by dying for us, justifying us by his blood, reconciling us to God, and saving us from His wrath. Because of the sacrifice of Jesus, we have peace with God.

In addition to acting as our peacemaker, Jesus told us how to handle conflict with other believers. If you sin against a brother, then go to him, admit your fault, and try to settle the matter (see Matthew 5:23–25). If a brother sins against you, then go to him, show him his fault, and try to get him to repent (see Matthew 18:15–16). In both cases, reconciliation is the goal.

Jesus also gave us a model for when to engage in conflict with people who are hurting others. His chief adversaries were the religious leaders of his day, who were abusing their authority and leading people away from God. Jesus confronted them, again and again, and then escalated the conflict after his triumphal entry into Jerusalem. He stormed into the temple, overturning the tables of the moneychangers and driving them out with whips. Then he went after the scribes and Pharisees, skewering them with parables and, in Matthew 23, calling down woes on them seven times.

The conflict ultimately cost Jesus his life. But it gave us salvation.

McKendrick's men nearly kill Emmett before Mal saves him. Mal is jailed and readied for a hanging. Jake and his nephew are kidnapped. Finally, Paden has had enough. But when Cobb threatens to harm Stella, the co-manager of the saloon, Paden is paralyzed into inaction.

Stella figures it out. "Cobb's using me to stop you. So good people are being hurt because of me. That makes me mad. Some people think because they're stronger, or meaner, they can push you around. I've seen a lot of that. But it's only true if you let it be."

Paden finally realizes that some conflict can't be avoided. To save his friends, and his adopted town, he needs to face his enemies.[14]

So do we.

PRAYER

Heavenly Father, give me courage when I should stand up for what's right, strength to stand down when I need to do that, and Your wisdom to discern my place in any conflict. Amen.

Questions for Reflection and Application

1. Why is it easier to keep the peace than to be a peacemaker?
2. What are some instances where you failed to act as a peacemaker? What happened as a result?
3. What is your gut reaction to conflict? Do you look for it? Try to avoid it? Why do you tend to respond that way?
4. What role does God play in your conflicts? How often to you pray before you enter a conflict? How can you involve God more fully?
5. With what people are you "at war" right now? What has led you to this point? What is your strategy for making peace with each person?
6. The Bible calls us to live in peace with other Christians. What are the characteristics of Christians with whom you find it difficult to live in peace? How can you overcome obstacles and make peace with them?

Discipline

Bible Passages

1. **Proverbs 3:1–12** – God disciplines those He loves
2. **Proverbs 5:7–23** – Discipline in sexual purity
3. **Job 5:17–27** – Blessed is the man whom God disciplines
4. **1 Corinthians 9:19–26** – Train to win
5. **Titus 1:5–9** – Church leaders must be disciplined
6. **Hebrews 12:3–11** – God disciplines you as a son
7. **Revelation 3:15–22** – God disciplines those He loves

Every athlete exercises self-control in all things. They do it to receive a perishable wreath, but we an imperishable.

—1 Corinthians 9:25

Pastor Kyle Idleman was in a bind. Easter Sunday was a few days away. Thirty-thousand people would show up to hear him preach, and he had no idea what to say. He wanted his message to be appealing, especially to people who rarely set foot in a church. So he did research. What did Jesus say whenever he had a large crowd?

Jesus said things that drove most of them away. He didn't want fans; he wanted followers. And being a real follower is tough.[15] It takes discipline. The kind of discipline that Herb Brooks demanded from every one of his players.

In 1979, Brooks took the helm of the US hockey team, which was essentially a collection of college players. Most people just hoped that the team wouldn't embarrass itself at the 1980 Winter Olympics. Brooks had higher goals. He didn't want to be competitive. He wanted to beat every opponent, including a Soviet "machine" that had won four straight Olympic gold medals. To have a shot, his team needed three things: cohesiveness, stamina, and toughness.

At tryouts, Brooks selected not the best players, but the twenty young men best able to contribute to team success. And he ran them ragged, at practices and in sixty-three exhibition games. "We may not be the best team, but we're going to be the best-conditioned team," he told them frequently.

This point was brought home, quite painfully, after a lackluster showing in an exhibition game in Norway. When the players got to the locker room, Brooks told them to get back on the ice for skate-sprints dubbed "Herbies," where one sprint was blue line and back, red line and back, far blue line and back, and goal line and back.

As the Herbies continued, the rink manager told the team they had to leave. Brooks replied to give him the keys and he'd lock up. When the rink manager turned off the lights and left, Brooks had the players skate in the dark. The team physician implored Brooks to stop for the players' health and safety. Brooks ignored him. With Brooks yelling "Again!" over and over, they did Herbies for an hour. After that experience, the players never gave Brooks another lackluster performance.

By the time it got to Lake Placid, the US team was, indeed, the best-conditioned team in the world. No opponent could skate with the Americans in the final period. Team USA used that stamina to stage a come-from-behind win in each of its first five games. Then it was the semifinals against the dreaded Soviets, who had beaten the Americans 10-3 in an exhibition less than two weeks earlier.

Before the game, Brooks looked at each player and said, "You are born to be a player. You are meant to be here. This moment is yours." Behind thirty-six saves from goalkeeper Jim Craig, the US team staged yet another comeback and, with a late goal by captain Mike Eruzione, won 4-3. Two days later, the team captured the gold in, of course, another comeback.[16]

Discipline is not the same thing as punishment. "Punishment looks back. It focuses on making payment for wrongs done in the past," write Henry Cloud and John Townsend in *Boundaries*. In contrast, discipline looks forward, with an eye toward helping us not repeat mistakes—or sins.[17] John Piper and others argue that, because Christ was punished for the sins of all believers, God does not punish believers; instead he disciplines "those he loves" (Hebrews 12:6).[18]

As the US hockey team discovered in Norway, the more you self-discipline, the less you have to be disciplined. But even the most self-disciplined person sometimes needs help from others.

Novak Djokovic had a reputation for being a talented tennis player with no stamina. He trained as hard as anyone but wilted in long matches. A doctor with little interest in tennis happened to witness Djokovic's collapse in the 2010 Australian Open quarterfinals and knew what was wrong. Six months later, the doctor connected with Djokovic and proved it: the player was allergic to wheat and dairy. Once Djokovic eliminated the allergens from his diet, he became one of the fittest players and rose to number one in the world[19], a position has he has held for more weeks than any other male tennis player in history.

In 1 Corinthians 9, Paul uses a sports analogy. Athletes train hard. They are self-disciplined. They compete. But only one wins, and his prize is fleeting. A Christian's prize, however, is everlasting.

How's your training going? Maybe you need to get back on the end line. Again!

PRAYER

God, I'm out of shape spiritually. Help me to accept Your discipline as well as coaching from other well-conditioned men. I may not like the training, but I'll do it. Amen.

Questions for Reflection and Application

1. Which is easier for you: discipline imposed on you by an authority figure or self-discipline? Which is more effective? Why?
2. Where has self-discipline served you well? Why has it worked there? Where has self-discipline failed you? Why has it not been enough there?
3. How has God disciplined you? What was the result?
4. Self-control is one of the fruits of the Spirit. How does the Holy Spirit enable you to be self-controlled?
5. In what areas of your life do you need more discipline?
6. How can you coach or mentor other men on being disciplined? Where do you need coaching or mentoring from other men?

Fatherhood

Bible Passages

1. **Genesis 17:1–8** – God promises to make Abraham a father of nations

2. **Exodus 18** – Moses receives help from his father-in-law

3. **Psalm 103:13–14** – God has a father's compassion

4. **Proverbs 4** – Solomon shares his father's wise instruction

5. **Matthew 1:18–25** – Joseph agrees to become the father of Jesus

6. **Galatians 4:1–7** – God adopts us as sons

7. **Ephesians 6:1–4** – Advice to children and fathers

"Is not this the carpenter's son? Is not his mother called Mary? And are not his brothers James and Joseph and Simon and Judas? And are not all his sisters with us? Where then did this man get all these things?"

—*Matthew 13:55–56*

Fathers often feel unappreciated. But their role is vital. "Fatherlessness is one of our top national social issues," says Joel Shaffer, the head of Urban Transformation Ministries. "Kids growing up without a father are four times more likely to live in poverty, nine times more likely to be raped or sexually abused, two times more likely to commit suicide, twenty times more likely to become incarcerated, and two times more likely to drop out of high school. Girls without a dad are seven times more likely to become pregnant as a teen."[20]

The vital role of being a father lasts a lifetime.

In the film *Parenthood*, Frank approaches his son Gil to ask for his advice. Gil is incredulous until Frank disarms him with this statement: "I know you think I was a [lousy] father . . . and I know you're a good father." The issue is that bookies are threatening to kill Gil's younger brother Larry unless he pays a debt of $26,000. Larry doesn't have it. Should Frank give it to him?

"You got that kind of money?" asks Gil.

"I got it, but it's gonna hurt," replies Frank. "I wanted to retire next year. This will put that off for a while. A long while."

After Frank shares that raising his children came with challenges, fear, and even pain, he adds, "You know, it's not like that all ends when [your child is] eighteen or twenty-one or forty-one or sixty-one. It never, never ends . . . there is no end zone. You never cross the goal line, spike the ball, and do your touchdown dance. Never. I'm sixty-four. Larry's twenty-seven. And he's still my son."

Later, Frank offers to help Larry, but only if Larry agrees to have Frank train him in the family business, paying the bookies over time. Larry opts to pursue a "big opportunity" in Chile instead. After Larry departs, Frank turns to Cool, the young, illegitimate son Larry had with a Vegas showgirl. Cool asks if his dad will be coming back. No, answers Frank. "Would you like to stay here with us?"

Frank will get another turn at fatherhood, this time with an adopted son.[21]

In the time of Jesus, Jews had no legal process of adoption. If a man died, his brother automatically became the head of his household. But adoption was important in the Roman empire. A Roman couple had the option of disowning a biological child but not an adopted child. If a child was adopted, then he or she became a permanent part of the family. That child received a new identity and, if he was a male, then he became an heir to the father and was viewed as fully united to him.

When Mary discovered that she was pregnant with Jesus, she was legally pledged to be married to a man named Joseph, but the two had not yet been wed. Joseph knew that he was not the father of the child in Mary's womb. If he made that fact public, then Mary could be stoned for adultery. Being "unwilling to put her to shame" (Matthew 1:19), Joseph decided to divorce her quietly. Then an angel appeared to Joseph in a dream and told him that Mary's child was conceived by the Holy Spirit and was the Messiah foretold by the prophets.

If he agreed to marry Mary, then Joseph would take her shame upon himself, because no one would believe that the child in her womb was conceived by God. In addition, Joseph would agree, in essence, to adopt the Son of God and raise him as his own son. Joseph did it, and his life became full of challenges.

The couple was not married in their hometown of Nazareth, where tongues certainly were wagging. Instead, they had to travel to Bethlehem, the home of Joseph's ancestors, for a Roman census. When they got there, no one would take them in, so the baby was born in a stable. After a year or two in Bethlehem, they were visited by wise men from the east, and then an angel warned Joseph to take Mary and Jesus and flee to Egypt to avoid Herod's slaughter of young boys in Bethlehem.

After Herod's death, the family returned to Nazareth. Mary and Joseph had other children, and Joseph provided for his growing family as a carpenter, training Jesus in his craft. It is likely that Joseph never lived down the shame of Mary's pre-marital pregnancy, and he died before Jesus started his ministry (see Mark 6).

The love of a father for his child—biological child, adopted child, stepchild—reflects God's love for us. God has adopted us as sons, sent His Spirit into our hearts, and made us His heirs (see Galatians 4:5–7).

Hang in there, Dad.

PRAYER

God, equip me and guide me to model my actions as a father—or father figure—after Your perfect example. Amen.

Questions for Reflection and Application

1. As the earthly father of the Son of God, Joseph had an incredible responsibility. How did he do it?
2. How do statistics on the positive influence of fathers encourage you?
3. How did your father do in his role as father? What things did he do that you want to (or have tried to) emulate? What do you want to (or have you tried to) do differently?
4. What other men do you consider mentors or role models for fatherhood? Why?
5. Thinking back to discipline (Week 3), how has God disciplined you as a son? If you are a father, then how have you disciplined your children? What was the result?
6. How can you help men who grew up without a good father or father figure?

Fear and Anxiety

Bible Passages

1. **Joshua 1:1–9** – God tells Joshua not to fear

2. **Isaiah 41:8–14** – Fear not! God is with you

3. **Jeremiah 17:7–9** – A man who trusts in God does not fear

4. **Matthew 6:25–34** – Do not be anxious . . .

5. **Matthew 10:16–23** – . . . even when you are persecuted

6. **Philippians 4:4–7** – When you feel anxious, pray

7. **1 John 4:17–19** – Perfect love casts out fear

And Jesus said to Simon, "Do not be afraid; from now on you will be catching men."

—*Luke 5:10b*

About eighteen months after their exodus from Egypt, the people of Israel arrived at Canaan, the land that God had promised to give to them. God told Moses to send twelve men, one from each tribe, to spy out the land. The spies were to ascertain how good the land was and how strong the people who lived there were.

After forty days, the spies returned. They brought back fruit, including a single cluster of grapes that was so large that it took two men to carry it on a pole between them. The land flowed with milk and honey, they reported to Moses, but the people there were strong and lived in large, fortified cities.

One of the spies, Caleb, stepped forward. He stated boldly that the Israelites could overcome the people there and should go and take the promised land by force, immediately. But ten of the other spies objected, saying that the inhabitants of the land were too strong. Then those ten went among their fellow Israelites and told them that the land was bad, even devouring its inhabitants. Worse, it was populated by giants, and the Israelites were like grasshoppers in comparison.

The ten spies were afraid. And they succeeded in making their fellow Israelites afraid. Joshua joined Caleb in trying to fight the fear. God had promised this exceedingly good land to the Israelites, he argued. If they refused to go in, he continued, the people would be rebelling against God. But it was no use. The people were ready to stone Caleb and Joshua until God intervened to save them (see Numbers 13–14).

The Israelites' fear cost them their opportunity. God made them wander in the desert for forty years, and all the adults who had resisted entering the promised land died in that desert.

Fear is an emotional response to the presence of danger. Anxiety is a state of uneasiness and apprehension about potential danger or uncertainty. The Bible doesn't speak highly of either.

In Matthew 6 and Luke 12, Jesus addresses anxiety by pointing out the obvious: nothing good comes from it. It doesn't add an hour to your life. (In fact, it probably reduces your lifespan.) God knows what you need, so focus on His kingdom, and He'll provide the rest. Jesus finishes with this: "Fear not, little flock, for it is your Father's good pleasure to give you the kingdom."

Some verses of David's psalms (such as 23:4, 27:1, 34:4, and 56:3-4) portray a close relationship with God as the antidote for fear. If you doubt that you can have a close relationship with God because you are too sinful, then the story of Peter's first encounter with Jesus may alleviate your doubt.

That first encounter was by the Sea of Galilee. A large crowd wanted to hear Jesus, and the only way Jesus could address everyone was to get into a boat and go a little offshore. A few fishermen's boats were there. Jesus chose the one owned by Peter, then called Simon, and taught the people from it. When Jesus finished teaching, he told Simon to go into deep water for a catch. After objecting that he had tried that already, Simon agreed.

His nets caught enough fish to fill two boats. Realizing who this man was, Simon fell down at the feet of Jesus and said, "Depart from me, for I am a sinful man, O Lord." "Do not be afraid," Jesus replied. By following Jesus, Simon – a sinful fisherman – would have the opportunity to catch men (see Luke 5:1–10).

Some Christians, citing passages such as Romans 8:15 and 2 Timothy 1:7, posit that fear and anxiety are sinful, evidence of a lack of trust in God. Other Christians, such as the Rev. Paul Grummond, Dean of Students at Moore Theological College in Australia, consider that viewpoint an oversimplification that can lead to destructive denial, guilt, and shame. The Bible, he says, offers compassion and answers, not condemnation.

When you have faith-related concerns, says Grummond, talking with your pastor can help you work through those. When you have deeper fear and anxiety issues, however, you likely will need more help than your pastor can provide. Getting professional help, such as therapy and prescription medication, is not at odds with the Christian faith, Grummond adds. After all, no one treats a broken leg purely with prayer and Bible reading.

"God is sovereign and in control, and you need to trust what He wants for you is better than what you want for you," says Grummond. "He's not going to leave you there. Keep going."[22]

PRAYER

God, You tell me not to fear or worry. I fear and worry anyway. Increase my faith! I give my fears and anxieties to You. Amen.

Questions for Reflection and Application

1. A rational fear can spur you to take necessary caution. How do you distinguish between a potentially constructive fear and a destructive fear?

2. The Bible says that we are to fear God. What is meant by that? How does the fear of the Lord differ from other fears?

3. NBA player Kevin Love got attention for admitting that he had anxiety attacks. Is there is a stigma for men who struggle with fear or anxiety? Why or why not?

4. If the antidote for fear and anxiety is a close relationship with God, then is the presence of fear or anxiety evidence that your relationship with God is broken? Why or why not?

5. A friend tells you that he is receiving counseling and taking medication for anxiety issues. How would you respond?

6. What steps can you take to trust more in God for the things in life that cause you stress?

Marriage

Bible Passages

1. **Genesis 2:18–25** – God creates woman for man

2. **Exodus 21:10–11** – A wife deserves food, clothing, and love

3. **1 Corinthians 7:1–5** – Intimacy in marriage

4. **1 Corinthians 7:12–16** – Hope for unbelieving spouses

5. **Ephesians 5:22–33** – Wives: respect. Husbands: love

6. **Colossians 3:18–19** – Husbands: love your wives

7. **1 Peter 3:1–7** – Advice for husbands and wives

However, let each one of you love his wife as himself, and let the wife see that she respects her husband.

—Ephesians 5:33

A successful marriage relies on conflict resolution. But nearly 70 percent of conflict in relationships centers on unresolvable, perpetual problems. How do you resolve conflict when you can't resolve the problem at its heart?

According to Dr. John Gottman, who has studied married couples for over forty years, a lot rests on how husbands and wives communicate during conflict. In stable marriages, there is five times more positivity than negativity during conflict; in unstable marriages, there is 25 percent more negativity than positivity. Repeated negativity during conflict can lead to corrosive negative behavior patterns—dubbed "The Four Horsemen of the Apocalypse"—that can doom a marriage: (1) criticism, presented as defects in the other's personality, (2) defensiveness, primarily to ward off a perceived attack, (3) stonewalling, or emotional withdrawal from interaction, and (4) contempt, which is the greatest predictor of divorce.

Husbands don't tend to bring up issues; wives do, 80 percent of the time. Once a "discussion" gets going, the husband is likely to react with more physiological stress than his wife, and he is much more likely to withdraw, or stonewall. That brings the conflict to a screeching halt and aggravates his wife.

Why do men and women approach and handle conflict so differently? Gottman and his team don't offer a lot of answers, but a blog post by a Certified Gottman Therapist offers a hint. In the post, the therapist describes a fight between his wife and himself in which she got critical. He got defensive and then withdrew. When his wife hugged him and said that she loved him, the words stung. "I *know* my wife loves me. What I really need is to know that she *likes* me. I need to know that she enjoys, respects, admires, and appreciates me."[23]

Citing the last section of Ephesians 5, Dr. Emerson Eggerichs posits that wives are wired for love, and husbands are wired for respect. In other words, wives love their husbands and crave love from their husbands; husbands respect their wives and crave respect from their wives.

How men and women feel during marital conflicts adds credence to Eggerichs' claims. When 7,000 people were asked whether they felt unloved or disrespected during conflict with their spouse or significant other, 83 percent of the men said "disrespected" while 72 percent of the women said "unloved." This mismatch in needs can lead to what Eggerichs calls the "Crazy Cycle."

A wife's primary need is that her husband loves her. When he does things that come across as unloving, her natural tendency is to motivate him to change. Because women tend to confront to connect, she will move toward him in what she perceives as a loving way and offer some constructive criticism about the ways in which he has been unloving. When his wife criticizes him, however, the husband may feel that she doesn't admire him or even like him. In his mind, criticism signals a lack of respect.

A husband's primary need is that his wife respects him. When she comes across as disrespectful, his natural tendency is to motivate her to change. If that triggers conflict with her, then he is likely to withdraw from the conflict. When he does, she may perceive this withdrawal or "silent treatment" as an act of hostility. In her mind, withdrawal signals a lack of love.

The way to stop the cycle is straightforward: the husband must love his wife, even if she is disrespectful, and the wife must respect her husband, even if he is unloving. Of course, this is easier said than done, but the Bible offers helpful tips.

Eggerichs points out that, in the New Testament, men are instructed to demonstrate *agape*—or unconditional, God-like love—to their wives, but women are not given the same instruction, because women already are wired to *agape* their husbands.[24]

In Ephesians 5, Paul explains to men what it means to *agape* their wives and challenges the men to do it "as Christ loved the church and gave himself up for her" (v. 25).

Similarly, God challenges women to demonstrate unconditional respect to their husbands, even when those husbands are not believers. "Likewise, wives, be subject to your own husbands, so that even if some do not obey the word, they may be won without a word by the conduct of their wives, when they see your respectful and pure conduct" (1 Peter 3:1–2).

Want a good marriage? Practice unconditional love and respect.

PRAYER

God, my wife needs to know that I love her. Spur me to lead by example, showing her love even when she doesn't show me respect. Amen.

Questions for Reflection and Application

1. How do you typically show love to your wife? How does she want you to show love to her?
2. Think of some times where your wife has wanted *agape* (unconditional love) and you have given her another type of love.
3. How does your wife show respect to you? How do you want her to show respect to you? How have you communicated that to her?
4. How do you respond when your wife does not show respect to you? How can you lead by example and show her love, even when she does not "fill your tank" with respect?
5. How can you and your wife have gentle, loving, respectful conversations about the love she craves and the respect you want her to show you?

Obedience

Bible Passages

1. **Genesis 22:1–18** – God rewards Abraham's obedience

2. **Deuteronomy 4:29–31** – God responds to obedience

3. **1 Samuel 15:22–23** – Obedience is better than sacrifice

4. **Jeremiah 7:23–29** – Obey God, and He will be your God

5. **Romans 5:12–21** – Adam's disobedience; Jesus's obedience

6. **Romans 6:15–23** – Become slaves to obedience

7. **1 John 5:1–5** – If you love God, obey His commandments

Do you not know that if you present yourselves to anyone as obedient slaves, you are slaves of the one whom you obey, either of sin, which leads to death, or of obedience, which leads to righteousness?

—Romans 6:16

F ew people get excited about being obedient. Fewer people got excited about singing in church before Isaac Watts came along.

Watts was not an inspiring figure. He stood all of five feet tall and sported a big head and a long, hooked nose. So, he devoted most of his life to writing. (Let the jokes about writers begin.)

When Watts was a teen, congregational singing in most English-speaking churches was deplorable. A deacon would read the first line of the song's text, and the congregation would respond by singing the rest in a slow and ponderous drone. A typical song had a crude text, such as this:

Ye monsters of the bubbling deep, your Master's praises spout;
Up from the sands ye coddlings peep, and wag your tails about

Challenged by his father to give people something better, Watts began to write hymns. For two years, he wrote a new one each Sunday. His early hymns, which were new metrical versions of the psalms, included "O God, Our Help in Ages Past" and "I Sing the Mighty Power of God." Later, he wrote the beloved Christmas carol "Joy to the World."

When he was thirty-three, Watts wrote a hymn that was controversial because it reflected his personal feelings, specifically about how the sacrifice of Jesus on the cross demands a response from us. The hymn became so popular and had such a big impact that theologian Matthew Arnold called it the greatest hymn in the English language. It was "When I Survey the Wondrous Cross." Its final verse explains what our response must be:

Were the whole realm of nature mine,
that were a present far too small:

Love so amazing, so divine,
demands my soul, my life, my all.[25]

One of Jesus's parables illustrates how obedience to God requires giving our all. A master who was going on a journey entrusted his property to his servants, "each according to his ability." He gave the equivalent of $5 million to one, $2 million to another, and $1 million to a third.

After a long time, the master returned and settled accounts with the servants. The first and second servant had doubled what the master had given them. To each, the master said, "Well done, good and faithful servant. You have been faithful over a little; I will set you over much." The third servant, however, had hidden his share of the master's money in the ground. Calling that servant wicked, slothful, and worthless, the master had him cast "into the outer darkness" (see Matthew 25:14–30).

Even when you know you should be obedient to God, it can be tough to stay on the path of obedience. God's chosen people demonstrated this, time and time again, in the Old Testament. For example, shortly after God rescued them from slavery in Egypt, the Israelites—tired of waiting for Moses to come down from Mount Sinai—made a golden calf and worshipped it. A generation later, the Israelites served God and were given control of the promised land, but after Joshua's death they abandoned God and ended up "in terrible distress" (Judges 2:15). Things were even worse after the reigns of David and Solomon. Israel split into two kingdoms, and the disobedience of the leaders (and the people) in both kingdoms ultimately led to their destruction.

Consistent obedience to God is not something that you can do on your own (see Romans 7). You need help. And God provides it, when you submit to Him.

After the Last Supper, Jesus had sobering words for his disciples, the men who had been his closest followers, and friends, for three years: he was going to die. Even though he would rise again, ultimately, he was going to leave his friends and return to his Father in heaven. But he wouldn't leave them alone.

God would give them the Holy Spirit, Who would act as a Helper, an Advocate, and a Counselor. The Holy Spirit would be with them, dwelling in them. He would teach them, reminding them of the teachings of Jesus. And He would act as the Spirit of Truth, guiding them in all truth (see John 14–16).

When you put your faith in Jesus, God gives you the same Holy Spirit. By relying on that Spirit, you can give God your soul. Your life. Your all. Every day.

PRAYER

Heavenly Father, sometimes I find it difficult to trust and obey. Help me to rely on Your Holy Spirit rather than myself. Amen.

Questions for Reflection and Application

1. Were you an obedient child? Why or why not?
2. Are you an obedient adult, when it comes to obeying the law and "following the rules" in the workplace and elsewhere? What laws or rules do you bend or break? Why? When is it hardest for you to be obedient?
3. Which of God's laws have you broken? Why did you break them?
4. God has given us free will and yet expects obedience. Why?
5. How can you improve on being obedient to God? What is your plan?
6. How would you respond to someone who says that Christianity is all about following the rules?

Patience

Bible Passages

1. **Genesis 37:12–36, 39:1–23** – Story of Joseph (part 1)

2. **Genesis 40:1–41:46** – Story of Joseph (part 2)

3. **Genesis 50:15–26** – Story of Joseph (part 3)

4. **Psalm 37:3–9** – Be still and wait for God

5. **Galatians 6:7–10** – Don't grow weary of doing good

6. **Philippians 1:3–14** – God will complete His work in you

7. **Hebrews 6:9–12** – Imitate those with faith and patience

And let us not grow weary of doing good, for in due season we will reap, if we do not give up.

—Galatians 6:9

"Baseball is grown men getting paid to play a game."

—from the film *Mr. Baseball*

God is faithful, but His timetable often doesn't match ours.

Ask Kurt Warner. He was a standout quarterback in high school, but no big college football program took an interest in him, so he went to Northern Iowa. For four years, including a "redshirt" freshman year, he did not get a chance to play. Finally, in his final year, Warner became the starting quarterback and led his team to an 8-3 record and a playoff berth. He was named the conference's Offensive Player of the Year. But no NFL team drafted him.

After a fruitless tryout with Green Bay, he went home to Cedar Rapids and took a night job stocking shelves at a supermarket for $5.50 an hour. A year later, he entered the Arena Football League and played three seasons with the Iowa Barnstormers. Then it was a season in Europe for a team affiliated with the NFL's St. Louis Rams. He signed with the Rams in 1998 but saw action in only one NFL game that season.

In the final preseason game of 1999, starting quarterback Trent Green suffered a season-ending injury, and the twenty-eight-year-old Warner became a starting NFL quarterback. He responded by recording the second-finest statistical season by a quarterback in NFL history and leading the Rams to a victory in the Super Bowl, where he was named Most Valuable Player.[26]

For every Kurt Warner, there are thousands of guys who are just as talented, train just as hard, and never make it to the big leagues.

And then there's John Lindsey.

He started in baseball's minor leagues in 1995. Sixteen seasons and 1,571 games later, he still was there. The thirty-three-year-old first baseman, who had a wife and young son in Mississippi, had never played a game in the major leagues.

In 2011, he was supposed to be "a good clubhouse guy" for the Dodgers AAA affiliate in Albuquerque. He was to anchor the middle of the order, drive in runs, and set a good example for the young guys. But he wanted more. He was too heavy, and his defense was suspect, so he changed his eating habits, lost twenty-five pounds, and got more agile. And he improved his hitting.

The result was the best season of his minor-league career. He vied for league leadership in batting average and slugging percentage. In August, he was hitting .380.

"If there's anybody that deserves to get a chance to play in the big leagues, it's John Lindsey," said teammate Jon Link. "Honestly, as much as I want to go to the big leagues, as much as I want to get called up to the big leagues in September, if it were between me and him, I'd say take him because he's earned it."

Lindsey finally got what he'd earned. In September, the Dodgers called him up. In his first MLB game he was called to pinch-hit against the Padres, but when the Padres changed pitchers, Lindsey was replaced by another pinch hitter. He got a chance to bat in the next game but flied out. A game later, he got a base hit.

That hit was his only one in twelve plate appearances. When the 2011 season ended, the Dodgers released him. He played for Detroit's AAA team for two years and in Mexican leagues for two more years, finally calling it quits in 2015. He never got back to the majors. But he really didn't care.

For twenty years, Lindsey made a living playing a game. A game that he loved. Weeks before he finally got his call to the majors, he said that he was at peace, even if that call never came. "I just really enjoy being at the ballpark every day. I don't know how much longer I'll get to do it, so I try to enjoy every second that I'm here and do everything I can to keep playing."[27]

His joy was in the journey. And that joy was infectious.

Your call is vital to the kingdom of God. You probably won't operate on a big stage. Instead, you'll toil in obscurity, unknown to anyone but a select few. And you may spend long stretches in the desert, wondering if you'll ever reach the sea.

He who began a good work in you will bring it to completion.

For now, He asks you to be patient. And enjoy the ride.

PRAYER

Lord God, You have the best plans for me. Forgive me when I demand my timeline instead of trusting in Yours. Thank You for being patient with me. Increase my patience with You and others. Amen.

Questions for Reflection and Application

1. When is it most difficult for you to be patient with other people?

2. When is it most difficult for you to be patient with God?

3. Why does God ask, or even require, you to be patient with Him?

4. Quite a few chapters of Genesis are devoted to the story of Joseph. Why? How was Joseph able to remain patient through many years?

5. To what role or roles has God called you in the past? To what role or roles is God calling you right now?

Praying

Bible Passages

1. **1 Samuel 1:9–20** – Hannah's fervent prayer

2. **Matthew 6:5–15** – Jesus teaches about prayer

3. **Matthew 7:7–11** – Ask, and you shall receive

4. **Mark 14:32–42** – Jesus prays in Gethsemane

5. **Luke 18:1–8** – The parable of the unrighteous judge

6. **John 17** – Jesus prays for his followers

7. **James 5:13–18** – The prayer of faith

"Or which one of you, if his son asks him for bread, will give him a stone? Or if he asks for a fish, will give him a serpent? If you then, who are evil, know how to give good gifts to your children, how much more will your Father who is in heaven give good things to those who ask him!"

—*Matthew 7:9–11*

Why do we ask other people to pray for us? Why do we pray for other people? Are we hoping that, if enough people bring the prayer to God, then God will do what we ask? If God had not planned the course of action for which we are praying, then will enough repetitions of the request cause God to change His mind?

In Malachi 3:6, God declares, "For I the LORD do not change." Biblical scholars agree that God cannot and will not change His character. In other words, He is who He is. Scholars disagree, however, on whether or not God can, and does, change His mind.

Those who believe that God's mind can be changed point to several Old Testament stories. In Genesis 18, Abraham asks God to spare Sodom and Gomorrah if there are ten righteous people there, and God agrees. In Exodus 32, Moses pleads with God not to "consume" the people of Israel, and God agrees.

In the book of Jonah, God instructs Jonah to go to the great city of Nineveh and tell the people there that, because of their evil, their city will be destroyed in forty days. After trying to escape God and being rescued by a big fish, Jonah arrives at Nineveh and delivers the message. The people there repent, and God decides not to do "the disaster that he had said he would do" (3:10). Jonah, who wanted Nineveh destroyed, gets really angry that God is "a gracious God and merciful, slow to anger and abounding in steadfast love, and relenting from disaster" (4:2).

Did God change his mind about Nineveh, and destroying the Israelites, and Sodom and Gomorrah? The Hebrew word that can mean "to change one's mind," *nacham*, can also mean many other things, including to be sorry, to have compassion, to comfort, to console, to regret, to relent, and even to repent. Some argue that, if God did change His mind based on our prayers or actions, then that would mean that God had imperfect knowledge.

Rather than changing His mind, God, in His perfect wisdom, may make some things contingent on our praying for them, so that we will turn our hearts to Him, rely on Him, and trust in Him. Another view on prayer is that its primary purpose is not to influence God but to change us. Prayer helps us get to know God better and, ultimately, brings our will in alignment with God's will.

In the psalms, David records that God heard his prayers and responded. Here are some examples:

- The LORD has heard my plea; the LORD accepts my prayer. (6:9)
- Blessed be the Lord! For he has heard the voice of my pleas for mercy. The Lord is my strength and my shield; in him my heart trusts, and I am helped . . . (28:6–7a)
- I sought the Lord, and he answered me and delivered me from all my fears. Those who look to him are radiant, and their faces shall never be ashamed. This poor man cried, and the Lord heard him and saved him out of all his troubles. (34:4–6)
- I waited patiently for the Lord; he inclined to me and heard my cry. He drew me up from the pit of destruction, out of the miry bog, and set my feet upon a rock, making my steps secure. (40:1–2)

In Luke 18:1–8, Jesus tells a parable on why we "ought always to pray and not lose heart." There was an unrighteous judge—he did not fear God or respect people. On a regular basis, a woman came to this judge and demanded justice against her adversary. For a while, he ignored her, but eventually she wore him down.

"I will give her justice," the judge said to himself, "so that she will not beat me down by her continual coming." Jesus concluded the parable by saying that God will give much speedier justice "to his elect, who cry to him day and night."

What if you're not praying for justice? What if you're praying for healing? Or a job? Or an end to hostilities with your wife, or your child, or your dad? Or some other issue or problem or need?

The Lord is at hand; do not be anxious about anything, but in everything by prayer and supplication with thanksgiving let your requests be made known to God. And the peace of God, which surpasses all understanding, will guard your hearts and your minds in Christ Jesus (Philippians 4:5b-7).

PRAYER

God, I don't fully understand prayer, and I don't pray nearly enough. Enlighten me and guide me so that my prayers become real conversations with my loving Father in heaven. Amen.

Questions for Reflection and Application

1. Make your case for or against each:
   a. It is possible to change God's mind/actions through prayer.
   b. God makes some things contingent on our prayers.
   c. We pray not to influence God but to bring our will into alignment with His.
2. Are your prayers monologues, or do you converse with God? How do you listen to Him?
3. Are any requests too small for God? Why or why not?
4. How do you react when God does not handle one of your requests the way that you want Him to? How should you react?
5. What does God want to hear in your prayers, other than requests?
6. For what other people do you pray? Who prays for you?

Serving

Bible Passages

1. **Joshua 24:14–28** – Whom will you serve?

2. **Psalm 100** – Serve the Lord with gladness

3. **Mark 10:35–45** – To be great, you must serve

4. **John 13:1–17** – Jesus washes the disciples' feet

5. **Galatians 5:13–14** – Serve one another

6. **Philippians 2:1–11** – The ultimate example of humility

7. **1 Peter 4:9–11** – Use your gifts to serve others

Do nothing from selfish ambition or conceit, but in humility count others more significant than yourselves. Let each of you look not only to his own interests, but also to the interests of others.

—Philippians 2:3–4

I got the call from my sister on a Sunday afternoon. An hour earlier, she had arrived at my mom and dad's house to find my mom in bed, unresponsive. My dad was in a state of shock. "Take her to the hospital!" he pleaded.

Her forty-year battle with a debilitating autoimmune condition was nearing its end.

I flew up from Florida on Monday and went straight to the hospital. At first, it seemed that my mom was rallying. But Tuesday morning, the lead doctor in the ICU gave us the news: her kidneys were failing. At first, he thought she might have a few days. An hour later, he told us to get everyone there as quickly as possible.

She died the next morning.

She had been a teacher her whole life. In her final hours, even when she was unable to speak, she still taught us. She taught us how to put others first and serve them. No matter what.

When her four children were young, my mom did everything for us. She made our clothes. Cooked us nutritious meals. Helped us with our homework. Attended our sports events, choir concerts, orchestra concerts, and all other events, even if we sat on the bench or had only a minor part. But her care for the welfare of others extended beyond her immediate family. Far beyond.

When my oldest sister was eight and I was two, my dad took a job in Oshkosh, Wisconsin, far from the only home my mom had ever known, Akron. She knew no one in Oshkosh, but still she ventured outside her new home—with her children in tow—to minister to strangers. She adopted a "grandmother" at the county home. She volunteered at the state mental hospital, talking to newly admitted women while painting their fingernails.

We returned to Ohio, but we never lived in Akron again. Instead, we lived in small towns, and my mom began to increase her service activities. She joined the church choir and a community choir, with her husband and children following her lead. When she learned of the devastation of the Hmong people of Laos after the Vietnam War, she led an effort to adopt a Hmong refugee family. She met them at the airport, helped them settle into a new home in a new country, helped the parents obtain employment, and even gave the parents driving lessons.

When my parents became empty nesters, my mom's level of service to others seemed to increase every year. She spurred her tiny church congregation to send over 2,500 quilts to Lutheran World Relief. The bookstore that she ran with my dad donated $50,000 worth of books to local schools. She coordinated a campaign to provide sturdy athletic footwear to hundreds of children. She led Rise Against Hunger events that prepared meals for thousands of people.

From her hospital bed, before she became unable to communicate, my mom continued to serve. Her last text messages and phone calls were to make sure that bills were paid and that others were able to take her place in various service organizations.

Her motivation, I believe, was a quote from St. Francis of Assisi: "Preach the gospel at all times. If necessary, use words." For most of her adult life, the one to whom she directed her unspoken preaching the most was my dad.

My mom always had an unshakeable faith in Jesus. My dad didn't. He had a lot of doubts. About twenty-five years ago, he walked away completely.

My mom didn't confront him or nag him about it. She simply modeled her faith for him. Quietly and consistently. After a decade, he started attending church with her again. And he realized that God had orchestrated their life together so that she could lead him to God.

He had said goodbye on Tuesday. And he didn't want to be there to watch his wife of sixty-two years die. It was too painful for him.

But he knew that she wanted him there at the end. She hung on until he arrived at the ICU around 8 a.m. Wednesday. As he held her hand, we gathered around her bed and sang hymns to her. Then we said our goodbyes.

And she got her crown of righteousness.

PRAYER

Lord God, Your Son Jesus modeled a life of service, to the point of giving his life as a ransom for many. Lead me to love others by serving them. Amen.

Questions for Reflection and Application

1. How does serving others flow from serving God?
2. When asked which commandment is the greatest (Matthew 22:34–40), Jesus cited Deuteronomy 6:4–6 (love God) and Leviticus 19:18 (love your neighbor). Who is your "neighbor"? (See Luke 10:25-37.) What are some ways that you can demonstrate love for your "neighbor" by serving him?
3. Why did Jesus wash his disciples' feet?
4. What are your strengths in serving others? How can you leverage them?
5. What are your weaknesses in serving others? How can you overcome them?

Suffering

Bible Passages

1. **Exodus 3:7–10** – God responds to Israel's suffering

2. **Isaiah 53** – The prophesied suffering of Jesus

3. **Luke 9:23–27** – Take up your cross daily and follow Jesus

4. **Romans 5:1–5** – Suffering leads to hope

5. **Romans 8:16–22** – Future glory will eclipse present suffering

6. **2 Corinthians 1:3–7** – When we suffer, God comforts us so that we can comfort others

7. **1 Peter 4:12–19** – How to suffer as a Christian

Blessed is the man who remains steadfast under trial, for when he has stood the test he will receive the crown of life, which God has promised to those who love him.

—*James 1:12*

For many of us, the apostle Paul's call to "rejoice in our sufferings" (Romans 5:3) seems absurd. When we experience suffering or see someone else suffering, we want the suffering to end. Now.

In his book *The Problem of Pain*, C. S. Lewis notes that, if suffering is good, then we should pursue it rather than avoiding it. He concludes that "suffering is not good in itself. What is good in any painful experience is, for the sufferer, his submission to the will of God, and, for the spectators, the compassion aroused and the acts of mercy to which it leads." The pain that suffering brings, wrote Lewis, is "God's megaphone to rouse a deaf world."[28]

When he wrote the book in 1940, Lewis was no stranger to suffering, but two decades later he experienced the most shattering grief of his life. Lewis was a bachelor into his fifties primarily because he could not find a woman who could understand, let alone match, his intellect. Then he met his equal in author Helen Joy Gresham, whom he called Joy, and the two became friends. When Joy faced deportation from England in 1956, Lewis married her, but the two lived in separate houses.

A few months later, Joy was diagnosed with bone cancer, and Lewis fell deeply in love with her. They were married by an Anglican priest in 1957, and Joy's cancer went into remission. It seemed that the pair would have many years of happiness, but in 1960 the cancer returned, and Joy died.[29]

A year later, Lewis wrote a book on grief that was so raw that it initially was published under a pseudonym. In it, Lewis cries out to God for answers on suffering and complains that he does not get a response. "But go to Him when your need is desperate, when all other help is vain, and what do you find? A door slammed in your face, and a sound of bolting and double bolting on the inside." Lewis concludes that God was not conducting an experiment on Lewis's faith or love "in order to find out their quality. He knew it already. It was I who didn't. In this trial He makes us occupy the dock, the witness box, and the bench all at once. He always knew that my temple was a house of cards. His only way of making me realize the fact was to knock it down."[30]

It's likely that Lewis was a bit hard on himself. Even Job, whom God called the most blameless and upright man on earth (see Job 1:8), had trouble with suffering, even regretting that he was born in the first place (see Job 3).

So, what are we to make of suffering? One of the choruses in Felix Mendelssohn's great oratorio *St. Paul* gives us insight.

The oratorio begins with Stephen, whom Acts records as one "full of grace and power" who "was doing great wonders and signs among the people," being opposed by some who claim that they had "heard him speak blasphemous words against Moses and God." In Acts, and in the oratorio, Stephen's enemies stir up the people, the elders, and the scribes, who seize Stephen, drag him before the council, and bring false witnesses against him. Stephen gives a stirring defense but, when he dares to accuse the people charging him (and their ancestors) of killing the prophets and the Messiah, they stone him to death, laying their garments at the feet of a young man named Saul, who approved of the murder. Saul, of course, became the apostle Paul.

Before continuing with the story of Saul, Mendelssohn inserts a breathtaking chorus with a hushed, *a cappella* climax. The words, based on James 1:12, are simple yet profoundly moving:

Happy and blessed are they who have endured,
For, though the body dies, the soul shall live forever.

Stephen knew that because he had been a faithful follower of Jesus, he would spend eternity in heaven. Paul grew to understand that too. After his conversion to Christianity, Paul endured great trials, which he lists in 2 Corinthians 11:23–27: imprison-ments, "countless beatings," thirty-nine lashes five times, three beatings with rods, a stoning, three shipwrecks, and danger from rivers, robbers, Jews, Gentiles, and many others. After writing 2 Corinthians, Paul was imprisoned for two years in Rome.

A few years after his release, Paul was imprisoned again. This time, his imprisonment would end with his execution. But Paul had remained steadfast through all his trials and, as he wrote in his second letter to Timothy, he knew that he would receive the crown of life, which God had promised to him.

He was happy and blessed. And he would be for all eternity.

PRAYER

Lord God, I don't rejoice in sufferings. I don't want to suffer. Pe-riod. Strengthen me when I suffer and help me to see suffering through Your eyes. Amen.

Questions for Reflection and Application

1. Why do faithful followers of God suffer?
2. Describe times when you have suffered. How did you see God at work during those times? After the suffering was over? What, if anything, do you wish that God had done instead?
3. When you are suffering, who or what brings you the great-est relief? Why?
4. On the first Good Friday, Jesus not only died for our sins but endured tremendous physical and emotional suffer-ing. Why? Why didn't he use his supernatural abilities to avoid some of the suffering? How would our world be dif-ferent if he had?
5. According to 2 Corinthians 1:3–7, your times of suffer-ing have equipped you to comfort others who go through similar suffering. Who can you comfort most effectively?

Temptation

Bible Passages

1. **Genesis 3** – Adam and Eve succumb to temptation

2. **Matthew 4:1–11** – The devil tempts Jesus

3. **Mark 9:42–50** – Don't tempt other believers to sin

4. **1 Corinthians 10:12–14** – God will provide a way of escape

5. **Galatians 6:1–2** – Help your brother without falling into temptation

6. **Hebrews 2:14–18** – Jesus helps those being tempted

7. **James 1:12–18** – Remain steadfast when tempted

For because he himself has suffered when tempted, he is able to help those who are being tempted.

—*Hebrews 2:18*

I don't do well with fasting.

When my kids were young, my wife and I did the annual World Vision 30 Hour Famine with members of the church youth group that we led. From lunch on Friday until supper on Saturday, participants didn't eat anything. On the Friday night of a Famine, my wife stayed at the church for a sleepover with the youth while I took our kids—who were too young to participate—home to sleep. I then made the kids breakfast and lunch on Saturday, before everyone reunited for a big supper Saturday evening.

When you are fasting, preparing food for others and watching them eat it is rough. It's especially rough when it's food you truly enjoy. I don't know why—and I'm not ruling out pure stupidity—but I tended to make my kids *really good* breakfasts on Famine Saturdays: cinnamon rolls, bacon, etc. The temptation to have just a bite was, shall we say, quite strong. But I resisted. Barely.

These days, I only fast when I have to, which is when I am having a "procedure" the next day. I try to schedule the procedure as early in the morning as possible, because an afternoon procedure lengthens the fast. I may be imagining it, but it seems that, during the long evening before I head to bed, every ad on TV and online is about food. Every one.

When my procedure is over, I am not interested in eating healthy. I just want to eat. A lot. I pigged out at McDonald's right after the last one.

Before Jesus started his three-year ministry, he was baptized. And then he did something odd. He went into the wilderness and fasted for forty days. *Forty days*. Not thirty hours. Not a few days. Not a few weeks. He ate nothing for over a month. At the end, "he was hungry" (Matthew 4:2). You think? I don't know how he functioned.

When Jesus was at his weakest, Satan came calling. In reality, though, Satan had been there all along, for the entire forty days. The previous verse in Matthew tells us that "Jesus was led up by the Spirit into the wilderness to be tempted by the devil."

Over the years, the devil has had good success with tempting people. His first effort, in the garden of Eden, was a home run from his perspective, and he has been honing his craft ever since. He knows our weaknesses. He tempts us when we are at our weakest. He exploits our vulnerabilities with the things that he offers. And he is a master at lying about the consequences.

Throughout a forty-day ordeal in the wilderness, and even at his absolute weakest point, Jesus resisted the devil. How?

Jesus relied on God and the truth of God's Word.

Satan started by tempting Jesus to convert stones to food, which Jesus desperately needed. Jesus replied with Deuteronomy 8:3. So Satan tried to use Scripture against Jesus. Taking Jesus to the top of the temple, Satan told Jesus to throw himself down, because God would send angels to protect him, preventing him from striking his foot against a stone (see Psalm 91:11–12). Jesus replied with Deuteronomy 6:16. Satan's final temptation was to offer Jesus all the kingdoms of the world if he would worship Satan. Jesus sent the devil away by quoting Deuteronomy 6:13.

Why did the Spirit lead Jesus into the wilderness to endure temptation while fasting for an unbelievable forty days? The writer of Hebrews tells us that, because Jesus "suffered when tempted, he is able to help those who are being tempted" (2:18). After explaining that Jesus is our high priest, that writer tells us this: "For we do not have a high priest who is unable to sympathize with our weaknesses, but one who in every respect has been tempted as we are, yet without sin" (4:15).

Temptation is not the problem. Giving in to temptation is. In 1 Corinthians 10, Paul provides examples of when the Israelites succumbed to temptation with disastrous results. These examples are for our instruction, he continues. "No temptation has overtaken you that is not common to man. God is faithful, and he will not let you be tempted beyond your ability, but with the temptation he will also provide the way of escape, that you may be able to endure it" (10:13).

Rely on God to endure temptation. And don't make cinnamon rolls when you're fasting.

PRAYER

God, temptation is everywhere. I need Your help to escape it or endure it. Make me strong. Amen.

Questions for Reflection and Application

1. The temptations of money and sex can lead men to risky and destructive behavior. Why are money and sex such powerful forces tempting men?

2. Eve ate the forbidden fruit in the garden because it looked so good, and Satan's lies tempted her. What forbidden fruits do you struggle to resist? Why are they forbidden? Why are they so tempting?

3. 1 Corinthians 10:13 often is misquoted to say that God will never give you more than you can handle. What's a better interpretation of the verse? What does God want you to do when you are tempted?

4. Recall a time when you gave in to temptation. How did God provide a means of escape or a way to endure the temptation without sinning? Why did you succumb to temptation anyway?

5. In Mark 9 (and Matthew 18), after telling believers not to tempt other believers, Jesus says to cut off your hand or foot or tear out your eye if it causes you to sin. What did he mean by that?

Work

Bible Passages

1. **Genesis 2:5–15** – God creates man to work the land

2. **Exodus 20:8–11** – Work six days, then rest on the Sabbath

3. **Ecclesiastes 9:7–10** – Enjoy life, love, and work

4. **Nehemiah 2:11–18** – Men decide to rebuild Jerusalem's wall

5. **Acts 20:33–35** – Paul's example through his work

6. **Colossians 3:22–24** – Work as if for the Lord

7. **1 Thessalonians 4:9–12** – Demonstrate a sound work ethic

109

For we are his workmanship, created in Christ Jesus for good works, which God prepared beforehand, that we should walk in them.

—Ephesians 2:10

"You still don't get it, do you? He'll find her. That's what he does. That's all he does! You can't stop him!"[31]

The Terminator was designed and built to perform one job. We were not. But we were created to work.

Before they retire, most men spend nearly half of their waking hours working. Your job is much more than your primary source of income. It's a big part of your identity. And it may not be offering you the fulfillment—or even the satisfaction—that you wish it did. In fact, according to results from annual surveys conducted by a think tank called the Conference Board, only about half of American workers are satisfied with their jobs.

Of the twenty-three job components that survey participants rank, the one that has the most influence on overall job satisfaction is potential for future growth. Other major influencers on satisfaction are communication at work, how workers are reviewed and recognized, and how interesting the job is. Wages ranked tenth out of the twenty-three factors, but men place more importance on financial factors than women do.[32]

In the days of Jesus, employers did not offer workers the many financial "benefits"—bonuses, raises, health insurance plans, retirement plans, stock options—that many of today's employers do. A typical worker was a day laborer who earned a day's wage for a day's work. He had to find a job every day, or he took no money home to his family.

In Matthew 20, Jesus tells a parable that compares the kingdom of heaven to a vineyard. At dawn, the owner of the vineyard looks for day laborers, finds some, agrees to pay each a denarius (a day's wage), and sends them into the vineyard to work. At 9 a.m., he finds others in the marketplace who have not found a job and tells them to work in the vineyard, offering to pay them "whatever is right." He does the same at noon and at 3 p.m.

At 5 p.m., the owner returns to the marketplace and sees men there who have not been hired by anyone. These men are desperate. There is only an hour left in the working day, and they are about to return home with nothing. The owner sends them to his vineyard to work. At least I'll earn something, each one thinks.

As the sun begins to set, the owner tells his foreman to pay the workers their wages, beginning with the ones who worked only an hour and ending with the ones who worked for twelve hours. To everyone's amazement, the ones hired at 5 p.m. get a full day's wage. But so does everyone else. This makes the workers who were hired at 6 a.m. angry, and they let the owner know. "These last worked only one hour," they tell him, "and you have made them equal to us who have borne the burden of the day and the scorching heat."

The owner replies, "Friend, I am doing you no wrong. Did you not agree with me for a denarius? Take what belongs to you and go. I choose to give to this last worker as I give to you. Am I not allowed to do what I choose with what belongs to me?" Jesus finishes with this: "So the last will be first, and the first last."

The kingdom of God is like this? How is that fair? It's not, unless there is joy in work.

Consider how the men who were hired at 6 a.m. felt . . . at 6 a.m. They knew that they would be working for twelve hours. They knew that they would bear the scorching heat of the early afternoon. They knew that they would earn a day's wage, and nothing more. And they were happy and at peace with all of that because they were assured that they were providing for their families.

At 6 p.m., all the men who had worked in the vineyard knew a few more things. The owner of the vineyard was true to his word. He was generous. He cared about people. The next time any of these men needed work—which was the next day—they would inquire with the owner of the vineyard. They would seek him out.

God works. He didn't stop when he finished creating everything. Instead, as Romans 8:28 tells us, God works every day, and He does it for the good of those who love Him and are called according to His purpose. We are the prized workmanship of God, and, as Ephesians 2:10 tells us, we were created to do the good works that God has prepared beforehand.

There is joy in work . . . when we work for God.

PRAYER

Heavenly Father, I thank You for working in me and through me, and I thank You for providing meaningful work for me. I ask that my work may honor You and bless others. Amen.

Questions for Reflection and Application

1. Describe your career path or paths. How did you end up on each of them? What career path do you regret not pursuing, and why?

2. In what situations and settings do you find the most joy in your efforts, and why? In what situations and settings do you find the least joy in your efforts, and why?

3. How do you feel when your work efforts seem to go unnoticed or underappreciated? Whose approval do you seek?

4. How do you support and encourage others in their work? How could you improve in that area?

5. How is your work/life balance? What changes should you make to have a better balance?

6. Why did God institute the Sabbath? Do you truly observe a Sabbath day, or a day of rest from your labors? Why or why not? What challenges do you face in resting from work?

Big Topics

B efore an entrepreneur starts a business, he spends a lot of time answering some critical questions:

- What problems will my product or service solve?
- Who has those problems?
- How many prospective customers are there in the market?
- How will I capture enough of them to get my business off the ground and turn a profit?

He looks at the big picture, and he thinks strategically.

If he gets the business going, then, a few years down the road, his focus shifts from strategic to tactical:

- What operational issues am I facing?
- How do I reduce costs?
- What do my current customers need?
- How can I keep them happy?
- What are my competitors doing, and how should I respond?

He doesn't have much time for a broad, expansive view, because the here-and-now has his full attention.

For many of us, the Christian life has a similar dynamic. When you first become a Christian, you spend a lot of time contemplating the big picture. What does this mean? How should I live? What changes do I need to make? A few years down the road, however, your focus shifts to day-to-day issues. Strategic takes a back seat to tactical.

This thirteen-week series will focus your attention on some big topics for Christian men. What does it mean to be courageous or to fight evil? What is your mission? What are your priorities? What rewards do you hope to gain? What is faith? What is hope? Why should you repent or forgive others? Why does God restore you? Give you strength?

You're not running a business. You're living a life.

Live it well.

Courage

Bible Passages

1. **Deuteronomy 31:1–8** – Moses: Be strong and courageous
2. **Joshua 1:5–9** – God to Joshua: Be strong and courageous
3. **1 Chronicles 28:20–21** – David to Solomon: Be strong and courageous.
4. **Ezra 7:27–28** – Ezra courageously returns to Israel
5. **Mark 15:42–47** – Joseph of Arimathea finds courage
6. **2 Corinthians 5:1–10** – An eternal perspective gives courage
7. **Philippians 1:18–26** – To live is Christ; to die is gain

Now when they saw the boldness of Peter and John, and perceived that they were uneducated, common men, they were astonished. And they recognized that they had been with Jesus.

—*Acts 4:13*

James, the brother of John, died first, executed with a sword. The other disciples met similar fates. Peter was crucified upside down, and his brother Andrew died on an X-shaped cross. Philip, Bartholomew, Thomas, Matthew, James son of Alphaeus, Thaddeus, Simon the Zealot—all were martyred. Of the eleven disciples who remained after Judas committed suicide, only one, John, died of natural causes.[33]

Why did anyone want them dead? Whom did they threaten?

After all, when Jesus was arrested, his disciples abandoned him. The boldest among them, Peter, denied three times that he knew who Jesus was. John was there at the crucifixion, but after that he and the rest went into hiding. Even after the risen Jesus appeared to them several times over a forty-day period, the disciples kept to themselves, out of the public eye. And when Jesus ascended into heaven, the disciples stared at the sky, hoping he'd come back.

Once they replaced Judas with Matthias, those disciples numbered twelve again—a dozen young, uneducated, common men with about 100 more around them. Their leader was gone. None of them had the courage to lead. Then God stepped in at Pentecost.

The house where the Jesus followers sat was filled with the sound of mighty rushing wind, and tongues of fire rested on each of the men. The disciples went into the streets to share the good news of Jesus, not just in their native language but also in the languages of foreign visitors to Jerusalem, who were astonished. Thousands of people gathered, and Peter boldly told them that God had raised Jesus from the dead and made him Lord and Christ.

In response, three thousand men became Christians that day. A few days later, when Peter healed a man who had been lame from birth, several thousand more became believers. Then Peter and John were arrested by the Jewish leaders. The next day, the two disciples faced the first real test of their courage.

The leaders asked the pair to explain the power or name by which they had healed the lame man. Peter boldly declared that the act had been done in the name of Jesus Christ of Nazareth, whom the leaders had crucified and whom God had raised from the dead. The leaders could not refute that a lame man had been healed, but they did not want Jesus proclaimed as a risen savior, so they told the pair not to speak or teach in the name of Jesus. Peter and John replied that they would be obedient to God and continue to speak of what they had seen and heard.

They, and other followers of Jesus, now had powerful enemies. Soon more disciples were arrested. They might have been killed if not for the intervention of the prominent Pharisee Gamaliel (see Acts 5). But the effects of the intervention didn't last long. A dispute between some Jews and a Christian named Stephen led to Stephen's execution by stoning. That sparked a great persecution against Christians in Jerusalem, with a Pharisee named Saul going house to house to arrest Jesus followers.

As Saul headed for Damascus to do the same thing there, he had a vision of Jesus and was struck blind. Three days later, he became a follower of Jesus and changed from persecutor to bold champion. After learning that the Jews in Damascus planned to kill him, Saul escaped the city at night and headed to Jerusalem to join the disciples there . . . but the disciples still feared him. So God stepped in again, this time through Barnabas.

Barnabas, who was trusted by the disciples, brought Saul to them and told them how Saul had converted and preached boldly in the name of Jesus. Then Saul went throughout Jerusalem and preached boldly there. When Jews sought to kill Saul, the disciples sent him to his home city of Tarsus. Inspired by Saul, who became the apostle Paul, the disciples and other Christian leaders acted with more courage, and the church grew.

And so did persecutions. The most outspoken Christian, Paul, endured imprisonments, beatings, whippings, a stoning, shipwrecks, and other hardships until he was beheaded. The other disciples did not fare much better. They and thousands of other early Christians chose tremendous suffering and often gruesome deaths over renouncing their faith in Jesus.

God gave them the courage to build the church. And the gates of hell will not prevail against it.

PRAYER

Jesus, for your sake, grant me the courage I need to stand, to act, and to move for that which is right and good. Amen.

Questions for Reflection and Application

1. Where have you witnessed courage? Describe what you saw.
2. Where have you exhibited courage? Describe what gave you courage, how you demonstrated it, and what happened as a result.
3. Where have you failed to exhibit courage? What happened as a result?
4. Winston Churchill said, "Fear is a reaction. Courage is a decision." In what situations would you need help from God to be courageous? How can you ensure that you will make the decision to be courageous?
5. In the Foreword, Kyle Idleman discusses encouragement. What men have encouraged you in the past? How did they do that? What was the result?
6. What men do you need to encourage? How will you do that?

Evil

Bible Passages

1. **Deuteronomy 30** – God gives life; evil brings death

2. **Psalm 141** – God, save me from evil!

3. **Isaiah 5:18–23** – Woe to evildoers

4. **Colossians 1:9–14** – God has delivered us from the domain of darkness

5. **2 Thessalonians 3:1–5** – God will guard you against evil

6. **1 John 4:1–6** – The Holy Spirit is greater than the spirit of this world

7. **Revelation 22:10–13** – Jesus is coming to judge the good and the evil

"In the world you will have tribulation. But take heart; I have overcome the world."

—*John 16:33b*

Chamberlain didn't see it. Churchill did.

In the mid-1930s, Adolf Hitler did little to hide his ambitions or intentions. He violated the Versailles treaty by ordering German troops to reenter the Rhineland. His government removed citizenship for German Jews, seized their property, and began to build concentration camps. He punished and even eliminated anyone in Germany who opposed him. His "police forces" were called "Legions of Death" and wore skulls on their caps.

He was an evil man set on world domination.

But after a 1937 meeting with Hitler at his lair in the Alps, the British foreign secretary convinced Prime Minister Neville Chamberlain that Hitler did not want war. Chamberlain adopted an approach of appeasement, or buying off Hitler with concessions. But the next year, Hitler annexed Austria and vowed to invade the German-speaking Sudetenland region of Czechoslovakia on October 1. On September 15, he agreed to meet in Munich with Chamberlain and the leaders of Italy and France to discuss a diplomatic resolution.

In three face-to-face meetings, Hitler told Chamberlain that Germany had no plans to expand beyond the Sudetenland. Chamberlain made careful mental notes about everything that Hitler said and did. Chamberlain's concerns about Hitler were calmed when Hitler gave him a friendly handshake with both hands. The gesture reassured Chamberlain that Hitler was in a sound state of mind and meant to keep the peace.

At the conclusion of the meetings, the four leaders agreed that Germany could have the Sudetenland, and Hitler also signed a non-aggression pact with Britain. Chamberlain assured Britain that the agreements with Hitler ensured "peace for our time."

Hitler, of course, had other ideas. In March 1939, he annexed the rest of Czechoslovakia. When the Nazis entered Poland, Chamberlain called for a declaration of war against Germany. The next year, Chamberlain was replaced as prime minister by Winston Churchill, who had been warning his countrymen about Hitler for years, such as in the 1935 essay *Hitler and His Choice*:

"[H]e makes speeches to the nations, which are sometimes characterised by candour and moderation. Recently he has offered many words of reassurance, eagerly lapped up by those who have been so tragically wrong about Germany in the past. Only time can show, but, meanwhile, the great wheels revolve; the rifle, the cannon, the tanks, the shot and shell, the air-bombs, the poison-gas cylinders, the aeroplanes, the submarines, and now the beginnings of a fleet flow in ever-broadening streams from the already largely war-mobilised arsenals and factories of Germany."

The man who never met Hitler saw the evil in the Fuhrer. The man who shook Hitler's hand and looked him in the eye missed it.[34]

Evil can be difficult to recognize. That's because Satan, whom Jesus called "the father of lies" (John 8:44), is a master deceiver. And so are the many demons who work for Satan, as C. S. Lewis posits in his classic book *The Screwtape Letters*. In the fictitious letters, the senior devil Screwtape gives advice to the less experienced Wormwood, who is tempting a man in London.

Two decades after the book was published, Lewis revealed that he pictured hell as a place where everyone is concerned about his own advancement and "lives the deadly serious passions of envy, self-importance, and resentment." When people asked how he was able to portray hell so well, he responded that he had a very reliable way of learning how temptation works: examining his own heart. Writing the book was easy for Lewis, but he never wrote with less enjoyment. Adopting Screwtape's diabolical attitude was not fun but "all dust, grit, thirst, and itch. Every trace of beauty, freshness, and geniality had to be excluded. It almost smothered me before I was done."[35]

Fighting the forces of evil—both seen and unseen—is not easy. Our adversary "prowls around like a roaring lion, seeking someone to devour" (1 Peter 5:8). Opposing evil is a battle in which we must engage. Every day.

God equips us for the battle with armor that enables us to "stand against the schemes of the devil" (Ephesians 6:11). God guards us against the evil one (see 2 Thessalonians 3:3) and ultimately, with Him on our side, nothing can stand against us (see Romans 8:31). That's because "he who is in you is greater than he who is in the world" (1 John 4:4).

PRAYER
Almighty God, guide me to recognize evil, and deliver me from it. Amen.

Questions for Reflection and Application
1. What is your definition of "evil"? How is it defined in the Bible?
2. Why can it be difficult to recognize evil?
3. Where have you witnessed the effects of evil forces at work in this world? How have these forces affected you or those you love?
4. What types of evil have been alluring or tempting to you? How have you resisted falling prey to Satan's lies?
5. How can you put on the armor of God to defend yourself against the schemes of the devil?
6. How can you help someone who is under spiritual attack?

Faith

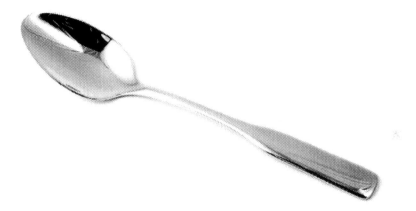

Bible Passages

1. **Deuteronomy 7:6–14** – God is faithful to His people

2. **Mark 9:14–29** – "Help my unbelief!"

3. **John 20:24–29** – Thomas doubts that Jesus is alive

4. **2 Timothy 4:6–8** – The result of a life of faith in Christ

5. **Hebrews 11** – The "Faith Hall of Fame"

6. **Hebrews 12:1–4** – Jesus is the founder and perfecter of our faith

7. **James 2:14–26** – Faith without works is dead

I have fought the good fight, I have finished the race, I have kept the faith. Henceforth there is laid up for me the crown of righteousness, which the Lord, the righteous judge, will award to me on that day, and not only to me but also to all who have loved his appearing.

—*2 Timothy 4:7–8*

After his body is unplugged, Neo begins to live in the real world. His previous existence was as part of the Matrix, a neural interactive simulation developed by machines. By keeping people's brains connected to this dreamworld, the machines are able to siphon power off the people's unused bodies.

The rebels who freed Neo have found a way to plug people back into the Matrix but enable them to be extracted when they wish. Those rebels take Neo with them into the Matrix so that Neo can visit someone called the Oracle. As Neo waits to see her, he observes a bald child bending spoons with his mind. "Do not try and bend the spoon," the child instructs Neo. "That's impossible. Instead, only try to realize the truth."

"What truth?" asks Neo.

"There is no spoon."[36]

Spoons do not exist in the Matrix. Nothing does. In the real world, however, bending a spoon with your mind requires bending an actual spoon with your mind.

It's impossible. Or is it?

After Jesus cast out a demon that gave a boy terrible seizures, the disciples asked Jesus why they had been unable to help the boy. "Because of your little faith," he answered. If you have faith then nothing will be impossible for you (see Matthew 17:14–20). He later added that "whoever says to this mountain, 'Be taken up and thrown into the sea,' and does not doubt in his heart, but believes that what he says will come to pass, it will be done for him.

Therefore I tell you, whatever you ask in prayer, believe that you have received it, and it will be yours" (Mark 11:23–24).

So, why aren't we moving mountains? Do we lack the faith?

Christian faith is faith in God—that is, trusting in God. When the disciples asked Jesus to increase their faith, he replied that they needed only a tiny speck of faith, the size of a mustard seed (see Luke 17:5–6). When we put our trust in God, we rely entirely on His great power and not on ourselves.

According to Bible scholar David Instone-Brewer, when Jesus mentioned moving a mountain, he was referring to "the mountain of the Lord," or the Temple. Shortly after the "mountain" reference, Jesus predicted that the Jewish leaders would be thrown out of "the vineyard" (see Mark 12:1–12) and that the Temple would be destroyed (see Mark 13:1–27), all within a generation (see 13:30–37). The predictions came true, in AD 70.

"Jesus wasn't telling his disciples to make showy or frivolous demands of God by moving mountains," writes Instone-Brewer. "He was teaching them to pray for the things that God has already said he wants to do to advance his kingdom." The scholar makes a similar argument for the phrase "whatever you ask in prayer," concluding that "we don't ask for whatever we feel like having: we ask for things that Jesus wants."[37]

But God wants what's best for you, right? So, why don't you get healing when you ask for it in prayer, with faith? Why does your wife leave, in spite of your prayers? Why can't your son get clean? Why are you stuck in this rut, year after year? Why continue to have faith in God when your prayers seem to go unanswered?

Hebrews 11 opens with this statement: "Now faith is the assurance of things hoped for, the conviction of things not seen." The rest of the chapter is called the "Faith Hall of Fame." It's a list of faith giants, men of whom the world was not worthy. Abel. Noah. Abraham. Moses. Gideon. David. Prophets. Many others.

Because of their faith, they accomplished amazing things. They "enforced justice, obtained promises, stopped the mouths of lions, quenched the power of fire, escaped the edge of the sword, were made strong out of weakness, became mighty in war, put foreign armies to flight." But some were tortured to death. Others were mocked, flogged, jailed, stoned, sawn in two. Wanderers. Cave-dwellers. Destitute. Mistreated in every way.

Regardless of what happened to them, none of them received what was promised to him. Not in this world. God had something better for them. Something that lasts forever.

They were ordinary men. Stubborn. Selfish. Fearful. Sinful. Knuckleheads. Men just like you and me.

What set them apart was a tiny speck of faith.

PRAYER

God, I don't want to throw mountains into the sea. I simply want to be a faithful follower of You. Show me the way of faith and lead me so that my works reflect my faith in You. Amen.

Questions for Reflection and Application

1. Hebrews 11:1 says that faith "is the assurance of things hoped for, the conviction of things not seen." How do you get that assurance and conviction?

2. After Jesus rose, Thomas doubted that Jesus was alive. When Jesus appeared to his disciples on a mountain (see Matthew 28:16–20), some of them "doubted." Why did the closest to Jesus have doubts? What changed their minds?

3. What doubts do you have about God? How do these doubts affect your faith? How can you overcome them?

4. What things has God done to strengthen your faith?

5. Is God faithful to you only if you are faithful to Him? Give some examples from the Bible and your own life to support your case.

Forgiveness

Bible Passages

1. **Psalm 103:10–12** – God removes our sins from us

2. **Mark 11:25–26** – Forgive, so that you will be forgiven

3. **Luke 6:37–42** – Forgive, and you will be forgiven

4. **Luke 17:3–4** – Forgive your brother every time he repents

5. **Luke 23:32–34** – On the cross, Jesus forgives

6. **Ephesians 4:31–32** – Forgive one another

7. **Colossians 3:12–13** – As God has forgiven you, you must forgive others

Put on then, as God's chosen ones, holy and beloved, compassionate hearts, kindness, humility, meekness, and patience, bearing with one another and, if one has a complaint against another, forgiving each other; as the Lord has forgiven you, so you also must forgive.

—*Colossians 3:12-13*

"To forgive is to set a prisoner free and discover that the prisoner was you."

—*Lewis B. Smedes*[38]

In the film *Spider-Man 3*, Peter Parker battles four foes: his friend Harry Osborn, who believes that Peter killed his father; Flint Marko, who killed Peter's uncle Ben and has been transformed into the Sandman; a new Spider-Man suit that amplifies the darker qualities of Peter's personality; and Eddie Brock, who obtains that suit and is transformed into Venom.

In the film's climax, Flint and Eddie team up to try to kill Peter. Just as Eddie is about to succeed, Harry sacrifices his life for Peter's and is badly wounded. Eddie is killed, and then Flint shows up—not to fight, but to talk.

"I didn't want this," says Flint quietly. "But I had no choice."

"We always have a choice," responds Peter angrily. "You had a choice when you killed my uncle."

Flint explains that he and his partner committed a robbery because Flint needed money to help his dying daughter. Flint didn't want to hurt Ben; he just needed Ben's car. But Flint's gun went off accidentally. "I did a terrible thing to you," Flint concludes. "I spent a lot of nights wishing I could take it back. I'm not asking you to forgive me. I just want you to understand."

Peter pauses, considering what he has done to Flint's partner, Eddie, Harry, and others. "I've done terrible things, too," he whispers. Flint turns to leave, then turns back. "I didn't choose to be this. The only thing left to me now . . . is my daughter."

"I forgive you," says Peter softly. A tearful Flint departs.

After rescuing His chosen people from slavery in Egypt, God instructed them that forgiveness of sins requires an atoning sacrifice. Before such a sacrifice could be made, however, the people needed to repent and return to God. This is reiterated throughout the Old Testament, including in Deuteronomy 30:1–3, Psalm 7:8–13, and Joel 2:12–13.

When Jesus taught, he added another requirement: if you want to receive forgiveness, then you must forgive.

After giving his disciples the Lord's Prayer, which includes a statement on forgiveness—"forgive us our debts, as we also have forgiven our debtors"—Jesus said, "For if you forgive others their trespasses, your heavenly Father will also forgive you, but if you do not forgive others their trespasses, neither will your Father forgive your trespasses" (Matthew 6:14–15).

Jesus knew that forgiving other people can be difficult. Sometimes, it's extremely difficult, especially when those people sin against us again . . . and again . . . and again.

The disciple Peter knew this, too. He figured that there had to be a limit on how many times we have to forgive someone, so he asked Jesus to specify the limit. Could it be as high as seven times? Not even close, responded Jesus. Try seventy times seven.

Jesus elaborated on this with a parable (see Matthew 18:21-35). A king settled accounts with his servants, including one who owed a ridiculously large sum (the equivalent of billions of dollars). There was no way the servant could pay even a small fraction of it, but the king had mercy and forgave the entire debt. As soon as he was forgiven, that servant found a man who owed him the equivalent of a few thousand dollars. When the man could not pay, the servant had him thrown in debtor's prison.

Informed of this, the king summoned the servant. "You wicked servant!" he shouted. "I forgave you all that debt because you pleaded with me. And should not you have had mercy on your fellow servant, as I had mercy on you?" The king threw the wicked servant in debtor's prison. "So also my heavenly Father will do to every one of you," concluded Jesus, "if you do not forgive your brother from your heart."

Mary-Jane cradles a dying Harry in her arms as Peter Parker arrives. "I should never have hurt you . . . said those things," says Peter. "None of that matters, Peter," replies Harry. "You're my friend."

"Best friend," agrees Peter, as Harry dies.[39]

PRAYER

Heavenly Father, forgive me for my sins against You and against others, even when I repeat those sins. Forgive those who sin against me, even when they repeat those sins. Lead me to demonstrate Your forgiving heart. Amen.

Questions for Reflection and Application

1. What sins against you are the most difficult for you to forgive?
2. Why does God make his forgiveness of us dependent on how we forgive others?
3. Jesus forgave people who did not repent. Should you do the same? Why or why not?
4. In Matthew 18:15–17, Jesus advises us on what to do when a "brother" sins against us. What is the goal of this approach?
5. If you have used the "Matthew 18 approach," then describe how that went. If you have been reluctant to use the approach, then explain your reluctance and how you can overcome it in the future.

Hope

Bible Passages

1. **Psalm 33:13–22** – We hope in God's steadfast love
2. **Psalm 71:1–6** – Hope in God every day
3. **Psalm 130** – Hope in the Lord!
4. **Romans 8:18–25** – We hope for what we do not see
5. **Romans 12:9–13** – Rejoice in hope
6. **Romans 15:1–13** – Christ is our hope
7. **Colossians 1:24–29** – Christ in you is the hope of glory

May the God of hope fill you with all joy and peace in believing, so that by the power of the Holy Spirit you may abound in hope.
—*Romans 15:13*

He was a gang member, covered in tattoos, almost sixty years old. He had been in prison since he was a teen. He'd never cried. Not when his mom died or when his dad died. Not once. Not until he heard a chamber music concert. Then he sobbed. "I'm overcome with emotion," he said. "I've had no control over my tears for the last two hours during the show. What is it?"

"It's the human heart," says Eric Genuis, a pianist and composer who performed the music that the man heard. Music is disarming, Genuis continues. It allows anyone to have an encounter with his own humanity, including painful memories buried for years. So Genuis strives to write beautiful music that communicates hope and to bring that music to places where people have little hope, such as rehab centers, prisons, and inner-city schools.

He has played nearly 1,000 concerts in prisons. About 2.3 million Americans are in prison, and across the US there are pockets of culture that revolve around prison. In those pockets, young people feel an inevitability about ending up incarcerated. "There's this whole population that is forgotten, that is abandoned," says Genuis. Throwing your life away in prison isn't a devastating idea because, emotionally and internally, you threw it away a long time ago. People have forgotten their humanity. It has little worth for them.

"I want to detour them from the idea that prison is just part of life," he says. Music is his change agent. Today's youth can hear anything they want, he continues, but they aren't aware of music that uplifts their humanity, stirs the awe and wonder and creativity in life, elevates them, and helps them see their dignity as a person. The right music "is a language that speaks to the heart, mind, and soul in ways words will never touch." It can elevate the mystery behind the person. Elevate the soul. When we have hope, he says, wonder for life triggers a desire to pursue that wonder.

In Romans 3, Paul paints a gloomy picture about our chances of making it to heaven when we die. "None is righteous, no, not one; no one understands; no one seeks for God. All have turned aside; together they have become worthless; no one does good, not even one. . . . Their feet are swift to shed blood; in their paths are ruin and misery, and the way of peace they have not known. There is no fear of God before their eyes." He finishes the thought with this: "For by works of the law no human being will be justified in his sight." It's a hopeless situation. Everyone sins. Everyone falls short.

But Jesus changes everything. The righteousness of God is available to any sinner. If you believe and have faith in Jesus Christ, then you are justified by God's grace "as a gift, through the redemption that is in Christ Jesus, whom God put forward as a propitiation by his blood, to be received by faith."

By the time we get to Romans 5, the news is even better. Because we have been justified by faith, we have peace with God, and we have hope of the glory of God. Even when we suffer, we can rejoice, because suffering produces endurance, which produces character, which produces hope, and hope never disappoints, because God has poured his love into our hearts.

No music can offer us this hope. Only God can. But music can point the way to God and hint at the hope that God offers to every person. After all, music is one of God's creations, and "his invisible attributes, namely, his eternal power and divine nature, have been clearly perceived, ever since the creation of the world, in the things that have been made" (Romans 1:20).

Genuis hears lots of stories after concerts at prisons, PTSD clinics, and other places with hurting people. One ninety-year-old prisoner admitted that he had been living with the pain and suffering that he caused when he was nineteen. "I've killed a lot of people in my life," said another. "After hearing this, I've had a higher encounter with my humanity. I'll never hurt another person again."

A young woman in a South Carolina prison said that she had forgotten what it felt like to be human until the concert. When she got out of prison, she wrote Genuis to tell him that the concert was the turning point. She now has hope.

These are stories of suffering, and redemption. "And who's not in need of redemption?" asks Genuis. "We all are, and we all should seek truth to do all we can to bring hope and to bring redemption to other people's lives."[40]

PRAYER

God, I live in a world that offers little hope, but this world is not my home. Stir in me the hope that I need and inspire me to draw others to trust in You. Amen.

Questions for Reflection and Application

1. The Hebrew and Greek words for "hope" in the Bible denote trusting and waiting expectantly. How do those definitions of hope differ from the type of hope typically mentioned in day-to-day conversations?

2. Why did the Israelites hope in God? Why did Paul exhort us to hope in Jesus?

3. What do you hope, or trust, that God will do for you in this life? Why do you have that hope?

4. Does music point you to God and the hope that He offers you? If so, then what musical pieces or types of music do that for you?

5. What other aspects of God's creation point you to God and the hope that He offers you? Why do those things kindle your hope?

Mission

Bible Passages

1. **Exodus 4:1–17** – God uses even the reluctant: Moses

2. **Judges 6:36–40** – God uses even the reluctant: Gideon

3. **Isaiah 40:1–11** – Isaiah proclaims the good news and tells us to do the same

4. **Matthew 28:18–20** – Jesus gives the Great Commission

5. **Luke 1:1–4** – Luke tells his mission

6. **Luke 24:13–49** – The road to Emmaus...and after

7. **Acts 1:6–11** – Stop staring at the sky! There's work to be done

"Go therefore and make disciples of all nations, baptizing them in the name of the Father and of the Son and of the Holy Spirit, teaching them to observe all that I have commanded you."
—*Matthew 28:19–20a*

I t's two days after the crucifixion of Jesus. Two of his followers, Cleopas and a friend, are still in a state of shock. They went to Jerusalem for what they thought might be the greatest Passover celebration since the Israelites were freed from Egypt. Instead, their world has crumbled.

Now, they are walking seven miles, from Jerusalem to their hometown of Emmaus. As they walk, they keep talking about what happened to Jesus, trying to make sense of it. They can't . . . until a stranger joins them on their walk.

He asks them what they are discussing. "Are you the only one who doesn't know what happened in Jerusalem?" they ask him. They then explain that Jesus of Nazareth was the Messiah, the one who was to redeem Israel. There seemed to be nothing that Jesus could not do. But when the chief priests and rulers delivered him up to be condemned to death, Jesus didn't resist. When they crucified him, Jesus didn't come down off the cross.

After some silence, the two speak again, in a hushed tone. They say that some women in their company claimed that Jesus's tomb was empty and that angels had told them he was alive. Some of the disciples confirmed that the tomb was empty.

The stranger says nothing. Why did they blurt it all out? Does he think they're delusional? They hold their breath and wait for his response. "O foolish ones, and slow of heart to believe all that the prophets have spoken!" he says. "Was it not necessary that the Christ should suffer these things and enter into his glory?"

What? What does that mean? Now they are even more confused! But the stranger is just getting started. He slowly and steadily steps them through all the Scriptures, beginning with Moses, and interprets everything in the light of what has happened to Jesus. With every word that he says, their hearts are burning. Can it be true? Was Jesus really the Messiah after all?

Before they know it, they have arrived in Emmaus. They slow up, but the stranger keeps walking, as if he is going much farther. They urge him strongly to stay with them, and he agrees. He enters a house with them, and they prepare to have an evening meal. As they gather around a table, the stranger takes the bread, blesses it, and breaks it.

And he vanishes. "It was Jesus!" they exclaim.

So, what do they do? They drop everything and run. Seven miles. In the dark. They run all the way back to Jerusalem.

There they find the disciples and other followers of Jesus. "The Lord has risen indeed, and has appeared to Simon!" says one. Cleopas and his friend tell the others what happened on the road to Emmaus, and how they recognized Jesus when he broke the bread.

Then Jesus appears, right in the middle of the room. They think he's a ghost, so he tells them to look at his hands and feet and even touch him. They want to believe it, but it's too wonderful to be believed.

So he asks them, "Have you anything here to eat?" Without thinking, someone hands him a piece of broiled fish. He takes it and eats it. That simple, everyday action breaks the tension, and the room is suddenly filled with laughter, tears, and shouts of joy.

Don't leave us again, each one thinks. But Jesus doesn't stay. He vanishes. And a few weeks later, he disappears for good, ascending into heaven.

His leaving was the best thing for them. And for us.

Consider the pair who walked to Emmaus. What would have happened to them if Jesus had stayed with them, as they wanted? They could have asked him a ton of questions. They could have celebrated with him long into the night. And the next day, they could have traveled with him wherever he went.

But they wouldn't have run from Emmaus to Jerusalem. They wouldn't have risked everything to share the good news.

Today, and every day, we need to catch the wonder of the risen Jesus, as they did when he broke the bread at their table. And when we catch it, we need to resist the urge to stay put and ask for more.

Instead, we need to run and tell others.

PRAYER

God, I'm tired of coasting. I'm tired of sitting on the sidelines. I need to get on the road, running from Emmaus to Jerusalem. Spur me on and give opportunities to share the hope that you have put within me. Amen.

Questions for Reflection and Application

1. What is your mission? How has God made you and equipped you for it?

2. When God called Moses, what excuses did Moses give? How did God respond?

3. Peter denied Jesus three times. After Jesus ascended, Peter preached boldly in Jerusalem, and 3,000 men became followers of Jesus. What caused this dramatic change?

4. Mark and Luke were not disciples, but each wrote a Gospel. How do you communicate best? How can you best use your gifts and talents to spread the good news?

5. What are the key differences between evangelism and making disciples? How can you do the latter?

Priorities

Bible Passages

1. **Exodus 20:1–11** – The first four Commandments cover our relationship with God

2. **Matthew 22:34–40** – The two greatest commandments

3. **Luke 9:57–62** – Following Jesus must be your top priority

4. **Acts 13:42–52** – Paul changes his strategy

5. **Acts 20:18–38** – Paul recaps the priorities of his ministry

6. **Philippians 3:12–16** – Press on toward the goal

7. **2 Timothy 2:22–26** – Be mature when setting priorities

"But I do not account my life of any value nor as precious to myself, if only I may finish my course and the ministry that I received from the Lord Jesus, to testify to the gospel of the grace of God."

—*Acts 20:24*

Rise up, O men of God!
Have done with lesser things;
Give heart and soul and mind and strength
To serve the King of Kings.[41]

Charles Hummel's booklet *Tyranny of the Urgent* became a bestseller because it recognized that most of us, when facing a choice between the urgent and the important, do the urgent. When we repeat that pattern over and over, we find that we rarely, if ever, have time for what is truly important.

The problem isn't a lack of time or even a lack of effort. The problem is priorities. How do we set them, or reset them, to ensure that we pursue what is truly important?

Like other Pharisees, Saul Paulus of Tarsus believed in the importance of God's law: both the written law, or Torah, and the oral law founded on the teachings of the prophets and the oral traditions of the Jewish people. He believed that true worship of God was not temple sacrifices but prayer and the study of God's law. And he believed that Israel's ultimate restoration was dependent on enough Jews doing what the Pharisees did.[42]

Saul's beliefs determined his priorities. In the recent past, a rabbi named Jesus had been a vocal, public critic of the Pharisees. He had challenged their belief system, called them hypocrites and blind guides, and told sinners that they were closer to the kingdom of God than Pharisees. The Pharisees had ensured that Jesus was killed, but his followers remained active and were spreading beyond Jerusalem. If they were not stopped, then Israel's hope of restoration with God could be threatened.

Saul's top priority was to stop them. He started by leading a persecution of followers of Jesus in Jerusalem. He went house to house, dragging off men and women to prison. Then, he obtained from the high priest permission to travel to Damascus, arrest Jesus followers there, and bring them to Jerusalem.

As Paul approached Damascus, his priorities got reset. Radically.

Blinded by a light from heaven, Saul heard a voice asking him, "Why are you persecuting me?" The speaker identified himself as Jesus and told Saul to go to Damascus and await further instructions. After three days, during which Saul did not eat or drink, a disciple of Jesus named Ananias laid his hands on Saul, saying that Jesus had sent him so that Saul could regain his sight and be filled with the Holy Spirit.

Immediately, Saul had himself baptized as a follower of Jesus. The man who had been persecuting Christians suddenly had a new priority: ensure that other Jews—even Pharisees—became Christians. After a few days spent learning all that he could about Jesus from Christians in Damascus, Saul went into the synagogues and boldly proclaimed that Jesus is the Son of God. He was so effective in Damascus that his former allies, the Jewish religious leaders, hatched a plan to kill him. Christians had to sneak him out of town at night.

Saul returned to his hometown of Tarsus, on the northeast corner of the Mediterranean Sea, and changed his name to Paul. After many years there, Paul decided to spread the gospel to the west. He started in Jewish synagogues, but it quickly became clear that most Jews would not accept his teachings and, worse, would persecute him.

So Paul changed his strategy. Rather than trying to convert Jews, he would try to get non-Jews to follow Jesus. For the rest of his life, the "Hebrew of Hebrews" (Philippians 3:5) became the apostle to the Gentiles.

Paul's priorities were reset twice: first on the road to Damascus and then on a missionary journey. Most of us would prefer to have a priority reset without being blinded or facing persecution. Is there an easier way to ensure that we're on the right path?

Hummel writes that Jesus had the right priorities because he took time to pray and get instructions from God. We can do the same. When we feel overwhelmed by life's demands, a time of prayer and meditation on God's Word can be like a time out in the final quarter of a close game. It enables us to catch our breath and get tips from our coach.[43]

And then we can make the right play.

PRAYER

Heavenly Father, I need Your help to set the right priorities so that I can live the life You want me to live. Enlighten me through Your Word. Amen.

Questions for Reflection and Application

1. What are your priorities in your career? At home? With your close and extended family? With your close friends? In your Christian faith?
2. How did you determine these priorities?
3. There are only so many hours in a day, a week, a month. Sometimes you have to choose between priorities in different areas of life. How do you prioritize among the different areas?
4. Write down your top ten priorities across all areas of your life. Now examine your list and narrow it down to your top five.
5. What would God's top priorities for your life be? How closely does that list match yours?
6. How do you know when you're on the right path?

Repentance

Bible Passages

1. **2 Chronicles 7:11–22** – When we repent, God forgives
2. **Jeremiah 5:1–17** – Israel refuses to repent and is punished
3. **Joel 2** – Return to the Lord your God
4. **Jonah 3** – The people of Nineveh repent and are saved
5. **Matthew 11:20–24** – Woe to unrepentant cities
6. **Luke 15:1–10** – Heaven rejoices when a sinner repents
7. **1 John 1:5–10** – Confess your sins, and God will cleanse you

From that time Jesus began to preach, saying, "Repent, for the kingdom of heaven is at hand."

—*Matthew 4:17*

Sheep have a reputation for being stupid. Some people argue that this reputation is unfair.

Blessed with keen eyesight, sheep are visual learners who can master certain tasks quickly, such as choosing a container marked with a certain color. Their senses of smell and taste enable them to identify beneficial and harmful plants, and good memory enables them to return to areas that offer good food. These memories can last for years: studies have shown that a sheep can recognize and remember at least fifty individual faces for two years or longer. Sheep are even smart enough that, if they are vulnerable to ticks, then they will avoid the lushest patches of vegetation where ticks tend to hide.[44]

Regardless of how intelligent they may be, sheep have a few tendencies that can result in behavior that is not terribly smart. The most troublesome tendency of sheep is their proclivity to wander. Even when a sheep is in the perfect environment, such as a lush pasture with fresh water nearby, it may, inexplicably, wander off. Because sheep tend to band together for protection, one wandering sheep can result in an entire flock wandering. And the path of the wanderers may lead right off a cliff.

That's what Turkish shepherds discovered in 2005, when one sheep went off the edge of a cliff, plunging nearly fifty feet to its death, and 1,499 sheep followed. Many of the sheep survived only because the bodies of early plungers cushioned the falls of the others.[45]

In the Old Testament, God's chosen people had a tendency to wander away from their shepherd (God), with disastrous results. In Isaiah 53:6, the prophet says, "All we like sheep have gone astray; we have turned—every one—to his own way."

When they wandered, the people, in essence, turned their backs on God. To be restored to a right relationship with God, they had to repent. That meant turning away from the direction they were heading and turning back to God. God told them this before they entered the promised land (see Deuteronomy 30). Whenever they returned to God, obeyed His voice, and followed His commandments, God promised to have mercy on them, forgive them, and restore them.

After they conquered and settled in the promised land, the Israelites began a vicious cycle of wandering away from God, struggling, and then returning to God. David's son Solomon, who prayed to God for wisdom, foresaw the pattern continuing. Your people are going to sin against You, he told God, and You will punish them with droughts, pestilence, plagues, military defeats, exile, and other afflictions. If they repent and turn again to You, Solomon continued, then please forgive them (see 1 Kings 8).

God responded, "[I]f my people who are called by my name humble themselves, and pray and seek my face and turn from their wicked ways, then I will hear from heaven and will forgive their sin and heal their land" (2 Chronicles 7:14).

The ministry and teachings of Jesus radically changed many things that Jews believed, but they did not change the relationship between repentance and forgiveness: first we repent, and then God forgives. When he prepared the way for Jesus, John the Baptist said, "Repent, for the kingdom of heaven is at hand" (Matthew 3:2). Jesus started his ministry with exactly the same words (see Matthew 4:17).

As the prophet Joel wrote, God is "gracious and merciful, slow to anger, and abounding in steadfast love" (2:13). To receive that grace and mercy, however, we must return to God. We must repent. "If we say we have no sin, we deceive ourselves, and the truth is not in us. If we confess our sins, he is faithful and just to forgive us our sins and to cleanse us from all unrighteousness. If we say we have not sinned, we make him a liar, and his word is not in us" (1 John 1:8–10).

God gives us plenty of opportunities to return to Him. "But do not overlook this one fact, beloved, that with the Lord one day is as a thousand years, and a thousand years as one day. The Lord is not slow to fulfill his promise as some count slowness, but is patient toward you, not wishing that any should perish, but that all should reach repentance" (2 Peter 3:8–9).

Sheep who have wandered, even a considerable distance, will turn around and come back when they hear the familiar voice of their shepherd. God wants us to do the same. And He's calling us now.

PRAYER

Blessed Redeemer, I don't deserve Your forgiveness, but I thank You that it is available to me when I repent. Amen.

Questions for Reflection and Application

1. Why does forgiveness require repentance?
2. Why did the people of God regularly wander away from God? How and why have you wandered away from God?
3. What is the difference between admitting that you sinned, confessing the sin, and repenting of the sin?
4. When you sin against someone, you can repent of the sin without making restitution (paying them in some way) for it. When do you think you should make restitution? How much should you pay?
5. Why did Jesus start his ministry with a call that everyone should repent and be baptized?

Restoration

Bible Passages

1. **Job 42:10–17** – God restores Job

2. **Psalm 51** – God restores the man who repents

3. **John 15:1–15** – Jesus is the vine; we are the branches

4. **John 21:15–19** – Jesus restores the failed Peter

5. **Galatians 2:16–21** – You are crucified with Christ

6. **Galatians 6:1–5** – Restore your fallen brother

7. **Revelation 21:1–5** – God makes all things new

Every branch in me that does not bear fruit he [lifts up], and every branch that does bear fruit he prunes, that it may bear more fruit.

—*John 15:2*

After sharing the Passover meal, Jesus and his disciples (minus Judas) left the upper room and began walking through a vineyard. There, Jesus used a vineyard analogy: God the Father tends the vineyard. Jesus is the vine. His followers are the branches. If the branches remain in the vine, they will bear much fruit, and God will prune them so that they will be even more fruitful.

As he began his analogy, however, Jesus said something troubling. Here it is in the New International Version: "He cuts off every branch in me that bears no fruit." Every branch in him is a follower of his, a Christian. Some Bible teachers interpret this verse to mean that, if a Christian bears no fruit, then he may not be a Christian after all. He may not be saved.

What if you don't produce fruit for a week? A month? A year? How long until God cuts you off?

Pastor Bruce Wilkinson wasn't comfortable with his understanding of this passage until he met a man who owned a large vineyard. As they sat over coffee, the man explained to Wilkinson the finer points of growing grapes. "New branches have a natural tendency to trail down and grow along the ground," he said. "But they don't bear fruit down there. When branches grow along the ground, the leaves get coated in dust. When it rains, they get muddy and mildewed. The branch becomes sick and useless."

Wilkinson asked the man what he does with a sick and useless branch. "Cut it off and throw it away?"

"Oh, no!" the man replied. "The branch is much too valuable for that. We go through the vineyard with a bucket of water looking for those branches. We lift them up and wash them off.

Then we wrap them around the trellis or tie them up. Pretty soon they're thriving."

After the conversation, Wilkinson realized that the Greek word *airo* in the passage never means "cuts off," as the NIV translation says, or "takes away," as some other translations say. The word should be translated as "takes up" or "lifts up". When a branch falls into the dirt, the gardener, God, doesn't throw it away or abandon it. Instead, He lifts it up, cleans it off, and helps it flourish again. God takes whatever steps are necessary to restore the branch.

For Christians, writes Wilkinson, sin is like mud trapping us on the ground. How does the Vinedresser lift us from mud? Sometimes, He must use painful discipline to bring us to repentance.[46]

Peter experienced this restorative discipline. Jesus had given Simon the name Peter, which means "Rock," and told him, "On this rock I will build my church." But at the Passover meal, Jesus told Peter that he would deny Jesus three times. Stunned, Peter replied that he would die with Jesus before he denied him. Just a few hours later, however, Peter denied Jesus three times—not to people in authority, but to servants and common people.

Peter was not a rock. He was a coward.

On Easter Sunday, Peter raced to the tomb and found it empty. Sometime later that day, Jesus appeared to Peter (see Luke 24:34) and then to all the disciples. But Peter still was swimming in guilt. He couldn't lead others; he could barely function.

A few weeks later, Peter decided to go fishing, and some other disciples joined him. They caught nothing all night. Early in the morning, a stranger on the beach told them to throw their nets on the right side of the boat. They caught 153 fish. The stranger was Jesus. Peter didn't know what to say to him, so Jesus did the talking.

Three times, Jesus asked Peter if he loved him. The third time, Peter was hurt and defensive. Jesus had opened a wound. But he had to, because otherwise that wound never would have healed.

Gently but firmly, Jesus told Peter that he would be a faithful follower from that point forward and would die for his faith.

Forgiven and restored, Peter became a new man. A new creation.

Like Peter, you can be reconciled to God and restored to what you were designed to be in the first place: the righteousness of God. Once you are restored, you can be what the restored Peter was: an ambassador for Christ, entrusted to share the gospel with others.

The Gardener is near, with His bucket of water in hand.

PRAYER

Create in me a clean heart, O God, and renew a right spirit within me. Cast me not away from Your presence and take not Your Holy Spirit from me. Restore to me the joy of Your salvation and uphold me with a willing spirit. Then I will teach transgressors Your ways, and sinners will return to You (Psalm 51:10-13). Amen.

Questions for Reflection and Application

1. How do you feel about Wilkinson's interpretation of what Jesus said in John 15?

2. In what areas do you need to be restored to God? How can you begin the restoration process?

3. What things have you done to others that have damaged your relationships with those people? What can you do to restore those relationships?

4. What things have others done to you that have damaged their relationships with you? What can you do to restore those relationships?

5. Should you try to restore a fallen brother (see Galatians 6:1-5) if he has sinned against someone else and not you? Why or why not?

Reward

Bible Passages

1. **Psalm 19:7–11** – Following God brings great reward

2. **Psalm 37** – God rewards the righteous

3. **Matthew 6:1–6, 16–21** – God rewards His servants

4. **Matthew 25:14–23** – Good stewards are rewarded

5. **1 Corinthians 3:7–15** – God rewards good works

6. **Colossians 3:23–24** – Serve Jesus in everything

7. **1 Timothy 6:17–19** – Be rich in good works

And he said to them, "Truly, I say to you, there is no one who has left house or wife or brothers or parents or children, for the sake of the kingdom of God, who will not receive many times more in this time, and in the age to come eternal life."

—*Luke 18:29–30*

Ray Kinsella has plowed up much of his cornfield to build a baseball field so that Shoeless Joe Jackson and the other disgraced 1919 Chicago "Black Sox" players can play their beloved game again. He has traveled to Boston to bring author Terrance Mann to the field. He has traveled to Minnesota to give "Moonlight" Graham a chance to step to the plate against major leaguers.

But when Joe invites Terrance, and not Ray, to the place in the cornfield from which the long-dead players emerge each day, Ray has had enough.

"Wait a second!" he blurts out. "Why him? I built this field. You wouldn't be here if it weren't for me." Over Terrance's objections, he adds, "I want to know what's out there. I want to see it."

"But you're not invited," responds Joe.

"Not invited? What do you mean I'm not invited?" objects Ray. "That's my corn out there. You guys are guests in my corn. I've done everything I've been asked to do. I didn't understand it, but I've done it. I haven't once asked what's in it for me."

"What are you saying, Ray?" demands Joe.

"I'm saying, 'What's in it for me?'"

Ray has sacrificed a great deal. How will he be rewarded?

The disciple Peter wondered the same thing.

A rich young ruler asked Jesus, "What must I do to inherit eternal life?" The answer: Sell all you have, give the proceeds to the poor, and follow me. When the man went away sad, Jesus said that it was easier for a camel to go through the eye of a needle than for a rich person to enter the kingdom of God. Peter noted that he and the other disciples had left their homes and followed Jesus (see Luke 18:18-28).

Peter had sacrificed a lot. In the future, he would sacrifice even more. How would he be rewarded?

On the night that Jesus was born in Bethlehem, the task of announcing the event was given to a "multitude"—hundreds or thousands—of angels. The Gospel of Luke says that the announcement was spoken, but it is possible that the angels sang the announcement.

Imagine that you are part of a chorus of angels that is going to deliver the biggest announcement in history. You have one shot. You need to do it perfectly. So you practice. A lot. Finally, it's time for the big performance, and your enormous chorus delivers the most important announcement in the history of the world . . .

. . . to a handful of shepherds. On a lonely hill. In the middle of nowhere. Was this a fitting reward for your hard work? Yes, for three reasons.

First, there is joy in performing well to any sized audience. While you certainly want the audience to enjoy the performance and to appreciate its quality, ultimately you are not performing for the audience. You are performing for God.

Second, your performance reached more than a few shepherds. The shepherds went and told Mary about it. Nearly sixty years later, Mary told Luke about it, and her description was so captivating that Luke recorded it in his Gospel. Hundreds of composers have put the event to music, and millions of choirs have sung about it to countless people. A performance to a handful, recounted to a single person . . . and we still hear the echoes over 2,000 years later.

Third, all of us will have the opportunity to watch the performance someday. Not just hear about it, but actually watch it. God didn't make a digital recording of it. He doesn't need to. He transcends time, and He'll give us the ability to do the same when we're spending eternity with Him.

Ray Kinsella's reward turns out to be this: one more chance to have a conversation, and a game of catch, with his estranged dad.[47]

Peter's was even better. Jesus promised Peter that he would receive "many times more in this time, and in the age to come eternal life" (Luke 18:30).

Jesus makes us the same promise.

PRAYER

Jesus, I try to follow you faithfully without thinking about what reward I may get but, deep down, I'd like to be rewarded, both now and in heaven. Thank you for understanding my desire and for promising me abundant life, now and forever. Amen.

Questions for Reflection and Application

1. What does it mean to lay up treasure in heaven?
2. How have you been rewarded already for your faith in Jesus? How do you expect to be rewarded during the rest of your life on earth?
3. What earthly rewards have you expected to receive that you have not received (at least, not yet)? Why have you not received them?
4. How much is your faith in Jesus dependent on the rewards you have been promised? How much of an influence should promised rewards have on a believer?
5. What do you think of Jesus's response to Peter in Luke 18?
6. Explain the parable in Matthew 25:14–30.

Strength

Bible Passages

1. **Psalm 29** – God gives His strength to His people

2. **Psalm 46** – God is our refuge and strength

3. **Isaiah 40:28–31** – God will renew the strength of those who wait on Him

4. **2 Corinthians 12:7–10** – Paul: "When I am weak, I am strong"

5. **Ephesians 6:10–17** – Be strong in God; put on His armor

6. **Philippians 4:10–13** – God supplies the strength you need

7. **Hebrews 4:14–16** – Jesus understands our weaknesses

In any and every circumstance, I have learned the secret of facing plenty and hunger, abundance and need. I can do all things through him who strengthens me.

—*Philippians 4:12b–13*

I f you were a distance runner a few decades ago, then your typical workout would consist of, well, running. You'd warm up, run, and then cool down. If you're a distance runner today, then your typical workout includes another element: core strengthening.

Research in the 1990s revealed that strength in your core muscles—the muscles in your abdomen, lower back, and pelvic area—is important for sports and fitness routines and even for everyday activities such as reaching and lifting. Before you move your arm or leg, you automatically contract your core muscles. When those muscles are strong, they stabilize your spine and provide a firm base of support for virtually all movement. They even enable you to breathe properly.

By transferring force throughout his body, a runner's core muscles prevent pain in his back, hips, knees, and neck. Strong inner core muscles help him stay upright while he runs, preventing him from wobbling slightly from side to side. His legs can do the work to prevent this lateral movement, but that takes away from their main job, which is to move forward, and slows him down. By enabling his joints and extremities to operate off a rigid structure, strong core muscles prevent pain in those joints and extremities.

A strong inner core also prevents common running injuries. A lack of stability in a runner's torso puts increased strain on other parts of his body such as his lower back, hips, and knees, eventually causing them to break down. Having more stability in his trunk also helps a runner deal with uneven terrain, making him less likely to fall or roll an ankle.[48]

The Bible talks a lot about strength. The word "strength" and variants of the word "strong" appear over 500 times. Often, the reference is to physical strength, as in the story of Samson.

That story begins with an angel telling a barren woman that she will have a son (Samson) who shall begin to save Israel from their overlords, the Philistines. To do this, Samson must be a Nazirite (see Numbers 6). A typical Nazirite would separate himself to serve God for a time, and during that time he could not cut his hair, eat grapes, or drink anything made from grapes. The angel says that Samson is to be a Nazirite his entire life.

As long as Samson remains a Nazirite, God gives him great physical strength, which enables Samson to tear a young lion to pieces with his bare hands, strike down thirty men with his hands, and strike down 1,000 with the jawbone of a donkey. But a woman named Delilah proves Samson's undoing. After she shaves Samson's head, God leaves him, and so does the strength that God provided.

Of course, physical strength is just one type of strength. We need it, but we need emotional strength and spiritual strength, too.

Late in his ministry, when he was in Rome, the apostle Peter wrote his first letter, directing it at Gentile Christians in Asia Minor. These Christians, like their brothers elsewhere, were being persecuted. Recalling the words of Jesus in Matthew 5:11–12, Peter's letter encourages them (and us) to rejoice when suffering. "After you have suffered a little while, the God of all grace, who has called you to his eternal glory in Christ, will himself restore, confirm, strengthen, and establish you" (1 Peter 5:10).

Emotional strength must be supplemented with spiritual strength. In Ephesians 6, the apostle Paul explains that "we do not wrestle against flesh and blood, but against the rulers, against the authorities, against the cosmic powers over this present darkness, against the spiritual forces of evil in the heavenly places" (v. 12). To win the battle, we need to "be strong in the Lord and in the strength of his might" and to put on God's armor (see vv. 10–11).

You have complete responsibility for strengthening your core muscles. To succeed, you need to understand your needs (the muscles that are most important for your sport or activity) and how to strengthen them (the exercises that are the most effective for those muscles). And, of course, you need to do the work.

God is the source of our strength for life, but you still have an active role to play. To be strong in the Lord, you must understand your greatest needs—where you are weakest and most vulnerable—and submit to God in those areas.

The more disciplined you are, the less likely you are to end up like Samson.

PRAYER

All-powerful God, I am not strong enough on my own, but Your strength can enable me to get me through any challenge. Teach me to rely on You for strength and provide me with what I need each day. Amen.

Questions for Reflection and Application

1. How strong are your spiritual "core muscles"? How can you get them stronger?

2. When have you relied on your own strength instead of turning to God? What was the result?

3. What does it mean to wait on God? What has been your experience with waiting on God?

4. No one knows what "thorn" made Paul weak (2 Corinthians 12:7–10). What "thorns" make you weak? Did God give them to you? Why or why not? How do you cope with them?

5. When it comes to following Jesus faithfully, what are your primary weaknesses?

Teamwork

Bible Passages

1. **Ecclesiastes 4:9–12** – Two or three are better than one

2. **Matthew 18:19–20** – A team can be just two or three

3. **Mark 6:7–13** – Jesus sends out twelve disciples in pairs

4. **Luke 10:1–20** – Jesus sends out 72 followers in pairs

5. **1 Corinthians 12:12–27** – You are part of the body of Christ

6. **Ephesians 4:11–16** – Leaders equip the saints to build up the body of Christ

7. **Colossians 4:7–18** – Paul praises his teammates

Now you are the body of Christ and individually members of it.
—*1 Corinthians 12:27*

Many sports fans like to debate who was the GOAT— "Greatest of All Time"—in a particular sport. Take men's tennis. Is the GOAT Roger Federer? Rafael Nadal? What about Novak Djokovic? Or Rod Laver, who twice won all four Grand Slam tournaments in a single year?

Basketball fans tend to narrow the GOAT debate down to Michael Jordan and LeBron James. But the debate is complicated by the fact that basketball is a team sport. The NBA championship trophy goes not to the best player but to the best team.

Even though he ruled for only nine years, Henry V made England one of the strongest kingdoms in Europe. Two years into his reign, when he was twenty-eight, Henry took his army to France. One-third of his men died of dysentery during a siege of Harfleur, and the remaining 6,000 faced 30,000 French soldiers at Agincourt. But Henry rallied his men, as immortalized by Shakespeare:

We few, we happy few, we band of brothers
For he today that sheds his blood with me
Shall be my brother, be he ne'er so vile,
This day shall gentle his condition:
And gentlemen in England now a-bed
Shall think themselves accursed they were not here,
And hold their manhoods cheap whiles any speaks
That fought with us upon Saint Crispin's day.[49]

With Henry fighting alongside his "brothers," the British won. The young king proved to be an inspiring leader and a solid teammate.

In life, you often team up with your closest friends. In a crisis, however, a team may be formed from total strangers.

After the success of the Apollo 11 and 12 missions, where four US astronauts walked on the moon, many people viewed Apollo

13 as a routine and even superfluous venture. That changed fifty-six hours after launch, when the spacecraft was nearing its lunar orbit. A routine maintenance task caused one of the craft's two oxygen tanks to explode. The explosion damaged the other oxygen tank and destroyed two of the craft's three fuel cells, which provided electricity and potable water to the astronauts. In two hours, all the breathable oxygen would be gone, and the astronauts would suffocate. Their lives were in the hands of Mission Control in Houston. NASA flight controllers and engineers had to find a way to keep the astronauts alive and get them home.

Houston started by ordering the crew to move from the command module, Odyssey, to the landing module, Aquarius, which had enough oxygen for four days, at which point they could transfer back to the damaged Odyssey for reentry into Earth's atmosphere. Engineers told the crew to turn off all non-critical systems to reduce energy consumption and to save water for cooling Aquarius's overtaxed hardware. When too much carbon dioxide was building up in Aquarius, Mission Control devised a way for the astronauts to build air filters out of plastic bags, cardboard, tape, canisters from Odyssey, and even an old sock.

Two more huge hurdles remained: (1) doing a burn to adjust their trajectory back to earth and (2) powering up Odyssey. Because there was no guidance computer in Aquarius, the burn required a concerted effort by the three astronauts and the team in Houston. The proper power-up sequence was devised by astronaut Ken Mattingly, who was scrubbed from Apollo 13 because he had been exposed to measles, and engineer John Aaron. Without the tireless work of many impromptu teams, Apollo 13 would have been not a "successful failure"[50] but a complete disaster.

The importance of teamwork is a regular theme in the Old and New Testaments. Recognizing that it was not good for man to be alone, God created woman, a "helper" who was "fit" for man (Genesis 2:18). Solomon noted that, just as iron sharpens iron, one man sharpens another (Proverbs 27:17). Jesus sent out his disciples in pairs, and the teams accomplished great things (see Mark 6:7–13 and Luke 10:1–20).

Paul, who always teamed with at least one other man on his missionary journeys, explains in 1 Corinthians 12 that each of us is a vital, even indispensable part of the body of Christ. The body can't function with division; it requires all its parts to work in harmony to accomplish its goals. To butcher a quote from Vince Lombardi, teamwork isn't everything, it's the only thing.

That's why it's pointless to argue about the GOAT in a team sport.

But I'm going with LeBron.

PRAYER

Jesus, you instructed your followers to minister in teams, and you sent them out that way. Lead me to teammates who make me more effective at your work. Help me to be a good teammate. Amen.

Questions for Reflection and Application

1. Describe at least three men who have been good teammates to you at key moments in your life. What made them good teammates?
2. Where have you been a good teammate? What are your strengths in teamwork?
3. Where have you struggled in teaming up with other people? What weaknesses do you need to overcome to be a better teammate?
4. In what situations do you prefer to be a team leader? Why?
5. In what situations do you prefer to follow the lead of someone else on the team? Why?
6. In what situations have you tried to go it alone, instead of partnering with others? How did that go?

Time

Bible Passages

1. **Psalm 90** – God, teach us to count our days

2. **Ecclesiastes 3:1–8** – For everything there is a season

3. **Isaiah 40:6–8** – People are like grass; God's Word is forever

4. **Ephesians 5:15–21** – Make the best use of the time

5. **2 Corinthians 4:13–18** – Fix your eyes on what is unseen

6. **James 4:13–17** – Life is fleeting; only God knows the future

7. **2 Peter 3:8–13** – Live today with eternity in mind

For this light momentary affliction is preparing for us an eternal weight of glory beyond all comparison, as we look not to the things that are seen but to the things that are unseen. For the things that are seen are transient, but the things that are unseen are eternal.

—*2 Corinthians 4:17-18*

Time, like an ever-rolling stream, bears all its sons away; They fly, forgotten, as a dream dies at the op'ning day.[51]

God is not bound by the constraints of time. But we are. And we wish we weren't. That's why manipulating time is a recurring theme in films.

In *Galaxy Quest*, after Brandon posits that the Omega-13 device is a matter rearranger that effects a thirteen-second time jump to the past, Gwen DeMarco asks, "Why thirteen seconds? That's really not enough time to do anything of any importance." Foreshadowing the film's climax, Jason Nesmith says, "It could be time to redeem a single mistake."

In *Back to the Future*, hours before he plans to travel back to 1985 from 1955, Marty McFly writes Doc Brown a letter warning Doc that he will be ambushed and killed by terrorists the night that he tests the time machine in the mall parking lot. But when Marty gives Doc the letter, Doc tears it up, and Marty must head off before he can warn Doc verbally.

"If only I had more time," says Marty to himself. "Wait a minute! I got all the time I want. I got a time machine! I can just go back early and warn him. Okay. Ten minutes oughta do it."

Thirteen seconds was enough time. Ten minutes wasn't.

In *Avengers: Endgame*, after the Avengers use time travel to undo the devastation wrought by Thanos—and then defeat him—Steve Rogers is assigned the task of going back in time to return the Infinity Stones to each of the locations from which they were "borrowed." When Bruce Banner tries to return Steve to the present day, however, Steve does not appear on the time travel platform. Two of Steve's friends then spot a man sitting a short distance from the platform, staring across a lake.

It's Steve. He's over 100 years old. Sam asks him what happened. "Well, after I put the stones back," says Steve, "I thought, 'Maybe I'll try some of that life Tony was telling me to get.'" When Sam spots a wedding ring on Steve's finger, he figures out that Steve, who fell in love in the 1940s, went back to that point in time to be with Peggy Carter, the woman he loved. The film ends with Steve and Peggy dancing . . . in the 1940s.[52]

Unlike Steve—and Jason, and Marty, and dozens of other fictional characters—we can't go back in time. Our existence on this planet is temporal, bound by the constraints of time.

But we do live forever.

His father and grandfather were Lutheran ministers, but young Joachim Neander had no interest in following God. Instead, he was a wild, rebellious, and immoral teen. When he was twenty, he joined a group of students who were ridiculing and scoffing at worshippers at St. Martin's Church in Bremen, Germany. The sermon that day, however, arrested him and led to his conversion. He began writing hymns, completing over sixty in the next decade.

At twenty-four, Neander became headmaster of a school in Dusseldorf. His strong Christian views and evangelical activities displeased the authorities there, however, and he was removed. Without a job and battling severe illnesses, he spent much of his time outdoors and even lived in a cave for a while. Then, at the age of thirty, he died of tuberculosis.

The year he died, Neander wrote his most famous hymn, "Praise to the Lord, the Almighty." Here is the English translation of the first verse:

Praise to the Lord, the Almighty, the King of creation!
O my soul, praise Him, for He is thy health and salvation!
All ye who hear, now to his temple draw near

Join me in glad adoration![53]

How could a relatively young man who was fired from his job, lived in a cave, and battled TB write such stirring words of praise? He fixed his eyes not on what is seen—his health, his circumstances, his troubles—but on what is unseen. He recognized that, while his time on earth was temporary, his life was eternal.

Living with eternity in mind won't enable us to go back in time. But it will make each moment count.

Starting now.

PRAYER

God, my life on earth is relatively short, but what I do here has eternal consequences. I ask Your Holy Spirit to guide my thoughts and actions, that I may bless others and lead them to You. Amen.

Questions for Reflection and Application

1. What does it mean to fix your eyes on what is unseen? How can you put that into practice?
2. How do you waste time? How do you justify it?
3. If we live forever, then why are our lives on earth so short?
4. What did Peter mean when he wrote that, for God, a thousand years are like a day, and a day is like a thousand years? How should that perspective affect how you live your life?
5. If you could go back in time and redeem a mistake that you made, which mistake would you pick? How does God want you to deal with that mistake?

Tough Topics

Sometimes, it's good to wrestle.

After spending the first forty years of his life as a momma's boy, Jacob finally left home, but only because his twin brother Esau wanted to kill him. Coached by his scheming mother Rebekah, Jacob had cheated Esau out of their father's blessing. To escape Esau's wrath, Jacob went to live with Rebekah's brother Laban, where he discovered that Laban was a master manipulator.

Jacob served Laban for seven years to earn the right to marry Laban's beautiful daughter Rachel, only to have Laban swap in his less attractive daughter Leah on the wedding night. To get Rachel too, Jacob had to commit to serving Laban another seven years. Rather than giving Jacob a dowry for his daughters, Laban continued to cheat and swindle Jacob at every turn, until Jacob and his family fled from Laban and set out for Jacob's homeland. On the way, they would have to meet Esau and 400 of his men.

Jacob was afraid. He asked God to deliver him but, hearing no response, Jacob decided to try appeasing Esau with a big gift, carried by Jacob's servants. Everyone in Jacob's party crossed the stream and headed for Esau, except Jacob. He stayed behind. And then a man came and wrestled with him.

The two wrestled all night. Neither could prevail. At one point, the man touched Jacob's hip socket and put his hip out of joint, but Jacob refused to yield. "I will not let you go unless you bless me," Jacob said. The man gave Jacob a new name: Israel, which means "he strives with God." And then the man blessed Jacob.

Suddenly, Jacob stopped worrying about Esau. The next day, the brothers met . . . and made peace.

In this thirteen-week study, you'll wrestle with tough topics. Some are issues with which men, Christians and non-Christians alike, struggle. Others are subjects on which Christians disagree and often have heated arguments.

My prayer is that, as you wrestle with these issues in the light of Scripture, you will be brought closer to God. Remember the words of Paul in his final letter: "All Scripture is breathed out by God and profitable for teaching, for reproof, for correction, and for training in righteousness, that the man of God may be complete, equipped for every good work" (2 Timothy 3:16–17).

Addiction

Bible Passages

1. **Psalm 34:15–22** – God delivers us from all afflictions

2. **Proverbs 3:1–8** – Trust in God; He will direct you

3. **Jeremiah 17:5–14** – Blessed is the man who trusts in God for everything, including healing

4. **Matthew 11:25–30** – Jesus's yoke is easy; his burden light

5. **Matthew 14:13–14** – Jesus interrupts his mourning to heal

6. **1 Peter 2:9–12** – As God's chosen, keep your conduct honorable

7. **1 John 2:15–17** – Love God, not the things of this world

Come to me, all who labor and are heavy laden, and I will give
you rest.

—*Matthew 11:28*

O ne of every ten American adults struggles with an addiction to drugs or alcohol. Drug overdose deaths are
increasing, and active addictions contribute to 70 percent of domestic violence incidents and 80 percent of child
abuse incidents.

Dan Gregory is not an addict. Furthest from it, actually. He
has no personal experience with drinking alcohol, taking drugs,
or even smoking cigarettes. After attending Christian schools, he
married his high school sweetheart and had six kids and a successful career. Then one of his sons began to struggle with drug
addiction, and Gregory decided to learn all he could about addiction treatment. What he found was a broken system.

"Addicts don't make rational choices," he says, "so there's
no quick solution to addictions. You need life transformation.
But treatment programs are driven by money, with the primary
question being, 'How do we get reimbursed?' There's no money
in long-term care, so most approaches are of the intensive, out-
patient variety. They treat addictions, not people."

The typical addict goes through a detox and then seeks treatment for his drug or alcohol addiction. If there is a gap between
detox and treatment, he is likely to relapse before he gets treated.

If his addiction is acute, then he will need three to six months
just to establish new learning processes, and he may need not
just rehabilitation but habilitation, or introduction to the basic
life skills necessary for daily functioning. A holistic year-long
program is needed, but most get treatment for just thirty days.
As a result, fewer than 20 percent of treated addicts are drug-free
after a year.

After several failures to get sober and stay sober, a man begins to lose hope that he ever will lead a meaningful, purpose-filled life.

Frustrated with what he found, Gregory approached his pastor for advice. The pastor offered a radical proposal: define the right solution, and the church will partner with you to build it. Gregory spent the next three years developing his expertise and his strategy by talking to dozens of people with experience and knowledge. Then he designed Restore Addiction Recovery, which opened its doors in 2021.

Restore views itself as a Christ-centered, Bible-based healing ministry. Its holistic approach lasts a year, but Gregory initially asks participants to commit for just a month. "For that first month, we let them breathe," he says. Residents receive love from the staff and hear about the love of Jesus. A lot.

"After the first month, it's eleven months of discipleship," Gregory continues. "And service." Part of that service is regular work at partner companies, which pay Restore, thereby enabling the program to be free for residents. The men work not just to learn vocational skills, says Gregory, but also "to bless others." Those "others" include the other residents. "Restore is for you. And you are for the others at Restore."

Restore wants men to do more than just defeat their addictions. Through integrated services, practical coaching and mentoring, and the building of healthy community, Restore empowers men to restore relationships, equips them for full-time employment, and prepares them to thrive in the real world. That's a world where they have failed so many times in the past.

But then again, so have we.

So did the apostle Paul, as he laments in Romans 7. No matter how hard he tried, Paul remained a slave to sin, one who didn't understand his own actions. He had the desire to do what is right, but not the ability, so he kept doing what he knew was wrong.

"Wretched man that I am!" he cries out. "Who will deliver me from this body of death?" (v. 24).

Only Jesus can do that. And Jesus does. Every day.

For Gregory, everything at Restore—and, frankly, everything in life—is about the first two verses of Romans 12. Every day, we need to present our whole selves as a living sacrifice to God. When we do, we are no longer conformed to this world, but we are transformed by the renewal of our minds.[54]

Addicts need transformation. So does everyone else.

PRAYER

God, I need Your transformation. I'm tired of repeating the same sins, over and over again. Fill me with Your Spirit and create in me a clean heart. Amen.

Questions for Reflection and Application

1. A man can be addicted to alcohol, illegal drugs, prescription drugs, nicotine, gambling, work, sex, pornography, or something else. What do all addictions have in common?

2. What are some reasons why a man becomes addicted to alcohol? Nicotine? Porn? Work?

3. How do people overcome addictions? What are the primary obstacles to complete addiction recovery?

4. Do you distinguish between an addiction and a vice? If so, what are the main differences?

5. What sins do you have that you keep doing, over and over? Are you addicted to this sinful behavior? If not, then why do you keep sinning? How can you stop?

Death

Bible Passages

1. **Exodus 12:1–31** – The Passover
2. **Job 19:23–27** – Job's redeemer lives
3. **Ecclesiastes 9:1–10** – Enjoy life while you have it
4. **John 11:1–44** – Jesus raises Lazarus
5. **1 Corinthians 15:12–26** – All will be made alive in Christ
6. **1 Corinthians 15:50–58** – Death has lost its sting
7. **2 Peter 1:3–11** – We are promised eternal life in heaven

Behold! I tell you a mystery. We shall not all sleep, but we shall all be changed, in a moment, in the twinkling of an eye, at the last trumpet. For the trumpet will sound, and the dead will be raised imperishable, and we shall be changed.

—*1 Corinthians 15:51–52*

Benjamin Franklin was the most-quoted public figure of his generation. The Founding Father—who was also a publisher, scientist, entrepreneur, and diplomat—recorded many sayings in *Poor Richard's Almanack* and his newspaper, *The Pennsylvania Gazette*. His last great quote came in a November 1789 letter that he wrote to French scientist Jean-Baptiste Le Roy. Franklin wrote the letter in French, but it was translated to English in 1817.

After inquiring about Le Roy's health and events in Paris for the past year, Franklin wrote this: "Our new Constitution is now established, everything seems to promise it will be durable; but, in this world, nothing is certain except death and taxes." He concluded by stating that he was growing thinner and weaker and did not expect to "hold out much longer."

Franklin died five months later.[55] His death was a certainty, just as yours is. The death rate for all of us is 100 percent.

But that certainty doesn't ease the pain when a friend dies.

John 11 tells the story of Lazarus. He and his sisters Mary and Martha were close friends of Jesus. One of the sisters sent word to Jesus that Lazarus was very ill. Rather than rushing to help his friend in Bethany, Jesus stayed where he was for two additional days. Then he told his disciples that Lazarus was dead, and they all headed to the home of Mary, Martha, and their dead brother.

By the time they got there, Lazarus had been in the tomb for four days, and his sisters were upset that Jesus had taken his time getting there. Both told him, "Lord, if you had been here, my brother would not have died." Jesus responded, "I am the resurrection and the life." And he raised Lazarus from the dead.

Before he raised Lazarus, however, Jesus wept:

When Jesus saw her weeping, and the Jews who had come with her also weeping, he was deeply moved in his spirit and greatly troubled. And he said, "Where have you laid him?" They said to him, "Lord, come and see." Jesus wept. So the Jews said, "See how he loved him!" (John 11:33–36)

Why did Jesus weep? Billy Graham had an answer.

"Death wasn't part of God's original plan for humanity," Graham said a year before he died. "The Bible calls death an enemy—the last enemy to be destroyed." Ultimately, death will be destroyed, Graham continued, and the resurrection of Jesus is the proof of this fact.[56]

Revelation 21:3–4 describes the time when death will be destroyed:

And I heard a loud voice from the throne saying, "Behold, the dwelling place of God is with man. He will dwell with them, and they will be his people, and God himself will be with them as their God. He will wipe away every tear from their eyes, and death shall be no more, neither shall there be mourning, nor crying, nor pain anymore, for the former things have passed away."

For now, we must deal with death. And dealing with the death of a loved one is difficult. Jesus demonstrated that he understood—and understands—this, and he offers us what we need: hope.

"The Bible tells us that Jesus Christ came into the world to give us hope—hope for a better life right now, and hope for life beyond the grave," Graham said. "We were meant for heaven, and when we open our hearts and lives to Christ in repentance and faith, we can have confidence that someday we will be with God forever."

Some people in the early church at Corinth did not believe in resurrection. In 1 Corinthians 15, Paul dismantles their arguments. He starts by reminding them of the basics of their faith: Jesus died for our sins, was buried, was raised on the third day, appeared to Peter and the other disciples, and appeared to more than five hundred others. If there is no resurrection, Paul continues, then Jesus could not have been raised; because he was raised, we will be, too. "For as by a man came death, by a man has come also the resurrection of the dead. For as in Adam all die, so also in Christ shall all be made alive" (vv. 21–22).

When we are raised, we will be changed, from mortal to immortal and from perishable to imperishable. Death will be swallowed up in victory, a victory that God gives us because of the saving work of Jesus. "Therefore, my beloved brothers, be steadfast, immovable, always abounding in the work of the Lord, knowing that in the Lord your labor is not in vain" (v. 58).

Death robs us of many things. But not our hope.

PRAYER

Death stinks, God. It just does. You know that—You sent Your Son to die. For me. Keep my perspective on death eternal and spur me to share the gospel with a sense of urgency. Amen.

Questions for Reflection and Application

1. The death of a loved one is tough. What is the most difficult death of a loved one that you have experienced? What made it so difficult?

2. Think about the memorial services and funerals that you have attended or witnessed in some other way (such as on television for a prominent public figure). What elements of those events have been the most memorable? Why?

3. People sometimes mention "a fate worse than death." What would be such a fate for you? Why would it be worse than death?

4. How would you like to be remembered at your funeral?

5. How can you live with eternity in mind? What should you be doing differently?

Divorce

Bible Passages

1. **Genesis 2:18–25** – The two become one flesh

2. **Exodus 21:10–11** – A wife has rights to food, clothing, and love

3. **Deuteronomy 24:1–4** – A potential cause for divorce

4. **Jeremiah 3:1–14** – God divorces adulterous Israel

5. **Malachi 2:13–16** – The "God hates divorce" passage

6. **Matthew 19:1–9** – The "any cause" discussion

7. **1 Corinthians 7:1–16** – Paul on marriage and divorce

"So they are no longer two but one flesh. What therefore God has joined together, let not man separate."

—*Matthew 19:6*

Once his divorce is finalized, a Christian man is likely to feel stigmatized by his church. After all, a good husband is not only faithful to his wife but loves her as Christ loved the church (see Ephesians 5:25). If the marriage failed, then it must have been his fault. Regardless of what happened, a divorced man is unable to serve in a leadership capacity in many churches, because every leader must be "the husband of one wife" (1 Timothy 3:2, 12 and Titus 1:6). And if a divorced man remarries, he may be accused of committing adultery.

Nearly 90 percent of Christian men leave their local church after a divorce. About 30 percent of them never find another church home.

But churches are just following the Bible, right? Didn't Jesus say that divorce is allowed only in the case of unrepentant adultery?

There are four passages in the Gospels that record Jesus speaking about divorce. It turns out that all four refer to the same conversation. When the Pharisees approached Jesus to talk about divorce, as recorded in Matthew 19, they asked him a very specific question, "Is it lawful to divorce one's wife for any cause?" Today, we interpret the question to mean, "Is there any valid reason for divorce?" But that's not the question they were asking.

A few decades earlier, a new form of divorce, called the "any cause" divorce, had been invented from a single word in Deuteronomy 24:1. A group of rabbis argued that you could divorce your wife not just if she was unfaithful but also for "any cause." She burned a meal? That's a cause. She wasn't as attractive as she used to be? That's a cause. Other rabbis disagreed with this interpretation of Deuteronomy 24:1, but the "any cause" divorce had become all the rage. The Pharisees, always keen to trap Jesus, were asking him this: Where do you stand on this issue?

Jesus's response (Matthew 19:4–9) is clear: the "any cause" divorce was a terrible interpretation of Deuteronomy 24:1. Men couldn't get a divorce for anything; they had to have a lawful cause. Because the "any cause" divorce was popular, many "divorced" people really weren't divorced. If they had gotten remarried, then they were committing adultery, because they still were married to their previous spouse.

Researcher David Instone-Brewer argues that Jesus not only defended the true meaning of Deuteronomy 24:1 but also accepted what the rest of the Old Testament taught on divorce. Exodus taught that everyone had three rights within marriage—the rights to food, clothing, and love. (We see these today in Christian marriage vows to "love, honor, and keep.") Paul taught the same thing: married couples owe each other love (see 1 Corinthians 7:3–5) and material support (see 1 Corinthians 7:33–34). If these rights were neglected, the wronged spouse had the right to seek a divorce. Abuse, an extreme form of neglect, also was grounds for divorce.

Of course, having grounds for divorce does not mean that one should divorce. God hates divorce, and for good reason. It can be devastating for all involved, and the negative effects can last for years. Divorce always should be a last resort. But God does allow for divorce—and subsequent remarriage—in some cases when marriage vows are broken.

In Biblical times, wives were dependent on their husbands for material support, and divorced (and widowed) women were in a precarious position economically and socially. A married woman would do everything she could to stay married and would consider divorcing her husband only if her husband was habitually unfaithful or was neglecting her, was abusing her, or had abandoned her. As a result, divorce was rare and always justified.

Obviously, things are different now. Divorce among US Christians is about as common as in the general population, and roughly seven out of ten of those divorces are initiated by women. For some of these divorces, there is a valid, Biblical reason for the divorce. But for some, there is not. In an era of no-fault divorce in every state, a healthy marriage takes the cooperation of two people, but a divorce takes the actions of just one.[57]

Divorced Christians need support and encouragement. Women often find it in the local church. Men often don't.

We can do better.

PRAYER

Father, divorced men are walking wounded among us. Help me to be sensitive to their struggles, to walk beside them in brotherly love, and to point them to you for comfort and restoration. Amen.

Questions for Reflection and Application

1. Would you attend a church led by a pastor who is divorced? Divorced and remarried? Why or why not? If your answer is conditional, explain the conditions.

2. How do you feel about the contention that Jesus's statements on divorce all stemmed from a question about the validity of an "any cause" divorce law?

3. Do you believe that Jesus and Paul affirmed what the Old Testament taught on divorce? Why or why not?

4. How much does a friend's current marital status and past marital history affect how you interact with him and treat him? Why?

5. Are Christian churches alienating divorced men? What should churches do differently? What can men's groups do differently? What can you do differently?

Equality

Bible Passages

1. **Matthew 16:13–20** – Jesus will build his church on an ordinary fisherman

2. **Matthew 27:45–53** – The temple curtain is torn in two

3. **Luke 23:55–24:11** – The women see Jesus put in the tomb Friday and see the empty tomb Sunday

4. **Acts 10** – Peter shares the gospel with Gentiles

5. **Galatians 3:23–29** – All are one in Christ Jesus

6. **Philemon 8–18** – Bondservant treated as a brother

7. **James 2:1–13** – Show no partiality

There is neither Jew nor Greek, there is neither slave nor free, there is no male and female, for you are all one in Christ Jesus.

—*Galatians 3:28*

Equality was a foreign concept in the Roman Empire. Men had a higher standing than women. Fathers had a higher standing than their children. Citizens had a higher standing than non-citizens. Those born free or made free had a higher standing than slaves.

First-century Jews had similar views on equality. They were the children of Abraham, God's chosen people, first in the eyes of God. Gentiles, or non-Jews, were inferior to Jews. So were Samaritans, who had their own version of Judaism. Among Jews, women had little standing—their testimony was not admissible in a court of law—and men's standing depended on wealth, family history, and other factors. At the top of the heap were those who kept God's law the best and thereby earned God's favor.

At first glance, it seems that Jesus shared these views.

He was a Jewish rabbi who said he "was sent only to the lost sheep of the house of Israel" (Matthew 15:24). When he sent out his twelve disciples, he told them, "Go nowhere among the Gentiles and enter no town of the Samaritans, but go rather to the lost sheep of the house of Israel" (Matthew 10:5-6).

But Jesus ministered to some Gentiles, including a centurion (see Matthew 8:5–13) and a Canaanite woman (see Matthew 15:21–28). Jesus also spoke at length with a Samaritan woman and spent two days teaching in her village, which resulted in many coming to faith there (see John 4:1–42). Later, he said, "I have other sheep that are not of this fold. I must bring them also, and they will listen to my voice. So there will be one flock, one shepherd" (John 10:16). After his resurrection, he instructed his followers to "make disciples of all nations" (Matthew 28:19).

Jesus focused on equipping Jews so that Jews could reach Gentiles. And that's just what they did. The first believers were Jews in Jerusalem who reached out only to Jews. Then believers began to reach out to Samaritans (see Acts 8) and Gentiles (see Acts 10). When Paul and Barnabas embarked on their first missionary journey, their goal was to reach Jews. But too many Jews opposed them, so they said, "we are turning to the Gentiles" (Acts 13:46). For the rest of his life, Paul sought to reach Gentiles.

Jesus treated women with dignity and respect that went far beyond the cultural norms of his day. He addressed women directly while in public, which was unusual for a rabbi—or any man—to do. (For examples, see Luke 7:12–13, Luke 8:48, Luke 11:27–28, Luke 13:12, John 4:7–26, and John 8:10–11.) When Jesus spoke to women, he used terms such as "daughter" and "daughter of Abraham" that gave them a spiritual status equal to that of men. And Jesus held women personally responsible for their own sin (see Luke 7:44–50, John 4:16–18, and John 8:10–11), demonstrating that women had the self-determination to deal with the issues of sin, repentance, and forgiveness.

Because Jesus demonstrated a high regard for women in both his life and his teaching, women responded warmly to his ministry. A significant number of early believers were women, and some played a prominent role in the early Christian church.

Paul, who had been a Pharisee before his conversion to Christianity, recognized that all Christians are equal in God's eyes:

[I]n Christ Jesus you are all sons of God, through faith. For as many of you as were baptized into Christ have put on Christ. There is neither Jew nor Greek, there is neither slave nor free, there is no male and female, for you are all one in Christ Jesus. And if you are Christ's, then you are Abraham's offspring, heirs according to promise (Galatians 3:26–29).

Equality, however, does not mean sameness. We each have a unique role to play, one for which each of us is uniquely designed. As Paul explains in 1 Corinthians 12, all Christians are a part of the body of Christ and each part is essential. But each part is different because God has designed each part—each person—to play a different role.

The challenge for a local church or other community of Christians is this: a well-functioning body relies on the harmonious interdependency of its parts. When a body is healthy, there is no division in it. Instead, the members care for one another. "If one member suffers, all suffer together; if one member is honored, all rejoice together" (v. 26).

How do you achieve harmony? You need to submit to God and to the leadership hierarchy that He has designed (see v. 28). And you need a more excellent way: the way of love.

PRAYER

God, we all are equal in Your eyes. You call me to consider others as more significant than I am. Help me to do that. Amen.

Questions for Reflection and Application

1. If everyone is equal in God's eyes, then why was Jesus sent only to the lost sheep of the house of Israel? Why did the disciples initially strive to reach only Jews?

2. What is meant by "first among equals"? Would Paul refer to apostles that way? Why or why not?

3. First-century women were not considered reliable witnesses, yet all four Gospels have women as the first eyewitnesses of the empty tomb. Does that fact help or hurt the credibility of the Gospels? Why?

4. Make a case that, because all Christians are equal in God's eyes and in the church, women should be allowed to hold the same church leadership positions—including pastor and elder—as men.

5. Make the opposite case: even though all Christians are equal in God's eyes and in the church, women should not be allowed to hold the same church leadership positions—including pastor and elder—as men.

Failure

Bible Passages

1. **2 Samuel 12:1–25** – David repents of his failure; God blesses him and Bathsheba with "beloved" Solomon

2. **Psalm 73:21–28** – When I fail, God is my strength

3. **Ecclesiastes 12:9–14** – Solomon's final words of wisdom

4. **Jeremiah 8:4–10** – When you fall, turn to God to rise

5. **Acts 15:36–41** – Paul and Barnabas separate over Mark

6. **Romans 8:1–11** – No matter how often we fail, we are set free in Christ Jesus

7. **2 Timothy 4:9–22** – In his final days, Paul asks for Mark

For I do not understand my own actions. For I do not do what I want, but I do the very thing I hate.

—*Romans 7:15*

Athletes strive to succeed, but some are known for their failures.

George Foreman was an angry man who wanted to hurt people. By channeling that anger, he became the most feared boxer alive. By the time he faced Muhammed Ali, Foreman was 40–0 with thirty-seven knockouts, including Joe Frazier and Ken Norton, the two fighters who had bested Ali.

Ali knew that going toe-to-toe with Foreman was suicide, so on a muggy night in Zaire Ali leaned back into the loose ropes around the ring. Again and again. Instead of pounding Ali into submission, Foreman wore himself out. In the eighth round, Ali ended the "rope-a-dope" and, with a few punches, knocked out Foreman. The unbeatable champion had lost the big fight.

After an eighteen-month hiatus, Foreman won four bouts, but he was no longer dominant or feared. When he was knocked out again, he dropped out of boxing.

During his first three NFL seasons, Earnest Byner had fewer rushing attempts than Cleveland's other running back, Pro Bowler Kevin Mack. But Byner was a better receiver, and his skills shone during the AFC Championship game in January 1988.

The Browns found themselves down 21–3 at halftime. Quick touchdowns by each team made it 28–10. Then Byner went to work. A key third down catch preceded a touchdown catch to make it 28–17. On the next Browns possession, Byner ran it into the end zone to make it 28–24. After a Denver field goal, Byner had a fifty-three-yard catch on a third-and-four. Six plays later, Cleveland tied the game at 31. Another Denver touchdown made it 38–31. The Browns had one more chance, with 3:53 left.

Byner ran for seventeen yards, then two. Two first-down completions to receiver Brian Brennan, a Denver offsides, and a Byner run gave the Browns a first down at the Denver 17. After an incompletion and another Denver offsides, Byner took a handoff, powered past the Broncos line, and headed for the goal line to tie the game. But he was stripped of the ball at the two-yard line, and the Browns lost.

Byner's name is forever linked with that play, known simply as "The Fumble." Browns fans couldn't forgive Byner, and after one more season Cleveland traded him to Washington.

The sports world may remember Foreman and Byner negatively for The Rumble and The Fumble, but the failures put the men's lives on new, very positive, trajectories.

After his failure in Zaire and his loss a few years later, Foreman had a near-death experience that caused him to accept Jesus as his savior. Rather than being driven by his anger, Foreman began to forgive people. He dropped out of boxing to begin preaching on street corners. He started and funded a youth and community center in Houston. Nearing bankruptcy, he came out of a ten-year retirement to raise money for the center by boxing, eventually becoming the oldest fighter ever to win the heavyweight crown.[58]

Byner won the Super Bowl with the Redskins in 1991, but something even bigger happened to him in DC. The team of that era was loaded with Christians, including Art Monk and Darrell Green, who befriended Byner. Another Christian, head coach Joe Gibbs, mentored Byner. In the middle of the Super Bowl season, Byner became a born-again Christian, baptized in Green's hot tub. He, Monk, and two other teammates founded the Good Samaritan Foundation to prepare youth in southeast DC, one of the roughest sections of any US city, for leadership in the community and the workplace.[59]

The Bible is filled with stories of failure. David committed adultery with Uriah's wife, got her pregnant, and had Uriah killed. His son Solomon married hundreds of foreign women and allowed them to turn his heart away from God. After Jesus was arrested, Peter denied three times that he knew Jesus, and the disciples abandoned Jesus and hid. Paul's anger caused a split with his closest ally Barnabas, and the two never saw each other again.

These stories, and many others, are there, in part, to remind us that failure does not have to define us. God can use our failures to teach us, and others, to rely more on Him.

Besides, the Browns probably would have lost in overtime anyway.

PRAYER

Father, I've failed before, and I'll fail again. I thank You that, every time I do, You pick me up and encourage me to get back in the game. Amen.

Questions for Reflection and Application

1. The Bible, especially the Old Testament, is loaded with stories of failure. Why are those stories there? Think of at least three reasons.
2. Think of some times when you have failed. What did you learn from each failure? How has God used each of them (other than to teach you a thing or two)?
3. In 1 Corinthians 15, Paul draws attention to his main failure, which causes him to call himself "the least of the apostles." In 2 Corinthians 12, he discusses his weaknesses. How do you feel when church leaders discuss their weaknesses and failures? Does that affect your respect for these leaders?
4. Should a spiritually mature Christian fail less often than a spiritually immature Christian? If your answer is "it depends," then list the dependencies.

Integrity

Bible Passages

1. **1 Kings 9:1–9** – God challenges Solomon to live with integrity
2. **Job 27:1–6** – Job vows to continue living with integrity
3. **Proverbs 2** – God protects those with integrity
4. **Ephesians 4:1–10** – Walk in a manner worthy of your calling
5. **Philippians 4:8–9** – Living with integrity is honorable
6. **1 Peter 3:8–17** – Have integrity, even during persecution
7. **Revelation 4, 5** – Jesus is worthy of our integrity

I therefore, a prisoner for the Lord, urge you to walk in a manner worthy of the calling to which you have been called . . .

—*Ephesians 4:1*

"You said you wanted to know how to get Capone," says beat cop Jim Malone to treasury officer Eliot Ness in the film *The Untouchables*. "Do you really want to get him? You see what I'm saying? What are you prepared to do?"

"Everything within the law," answers Ness.

"And then what are you prepared to do?" Malone continues. "Here's how you get Capone: He pulls a knife, you pull a gun. He sends one of yours to hospital, you send one of his to the morgue! That's the Chicago way! And that's how you get Capone."

Ness tries to stay within the law, but his resolve wavers after Malone is murdered. When one of Capone's men, Nitti, tries to escape from law enforcement at Capone's trial, Ness captures Nitti on the courthouse roof. When he realizes that Nitti killed Malone, Ness promises Nitti justice, according to the law, for committing murder. "Your friend died screaming like a stuck Irish pig," Nitti replies. "Now you think about that when I beat the rap."

Ness throws Nitti off the roof, and he dies on the street below.

Unlike Ness, early Christians were known for their integrity. They refused to renounce their faith, even when refusal meant death. Persecution actually emboldened Christians. For example, Paul's imprisonment gave most Christians confidence in God and made them "much more bold to speak the word without fear" (Philippians 1:14). 150 years later, the apologist Tertullian wrote, "The oftener we are mown down by you, the more in number we grow; the blood of Christians is seed."

Justin Martyr lost his life during the reign of Marcus Aurelius (AD 161–180). Aurelius noted that Christians remained resolute, even in the face of suffering and death. Aurelius respected others who maintained their principles and died for something significant, but he had no respect for Christians because he thought that they were disgustingly superstitious and perversely obstinate. Christians went to their executions with a willingness so extreme that he considered it theatrical display.[60]

After the first century, no eyewitnesses to the ministry, death, and resurrection of Jesus were still alive. The unshakeable faith of Christians relied upon the veracity of the four gospels, the letters of Paul, and the other letters that eventually were canonized as the New Testament. Early Christians trusted these documents because the authors demonstrated that they had written with integrity. Here are some examples:

- "And they compelled a passerby, Simon of Cyrene, who was coming in from the country, the father of Alexander and Rufus, to carry his cross" (Mark 15:21). Mark is saying, in essence, that Simon is dead but readers can verify the event with Simon's sons, who are still alive.
- "An orderly account" (Luke 1:3). After traveling with Paul and interviewing many believers, the physician Luke wrote two evidence-loaded letters—Luke and Acts—so that Theophilus could be certain that what he had been taught was true.
- "For I delivered to you as of first importance what I also received" (1 Corinthians 15:3). Paul met with Peter and other disciples several times and received the gospel from these eyewitnesses.

Back in the courtroom, Ness discovers that the jury in the Capone case has been bribed. He and the attorneys meet with the judge in his chambers, and the prosecutors show the judge a payoff sheet. "This constitutes no evidence," the judge says.

"Your Honor, the truth is that Capone is a killer and he will go free," says Ness. "There is only one way to deal with such men, and that is hunt them down. I have. I have forsworn myself. I have broken every law I swore to defend. I have become what I beheld and I am content that I have done right." Ness then asks to speak privately with the judge. Minutes later, the judge replaces the jury with one from another courtroom.

"What did you tell him?" the prosecuting attorney asks Ness. Ness replies that he told the judge that Capone's ledger of paid-off officials included the judge's name. "His name wasn't in the ledger!" says the attorney.[61]

The price of putting Capone away was Ness's integrity. We don't need to pay that price. Like the early Christians, we can trust the veracity of the Bible and live lives of integrity that mirror theirs.

PRAYER

God, You call me to live with integrity. Give me the strength and discernment I need to do that, every day. Amen.

Questions for Reflection and Application

1. Are there circumstances in which "the ends justify the means," even when those means are illegal or unethical? If so, then give some examples and explain why. If not, then how do we cope with the consequences of alternative ends, such as evil people hurting innocent people?

2. What was the result of early Christians living with integrity, even when they were persecuted and killed?

3. How can you demonstrate similar integrity today?

4. In what situations do you find it most difficult to maintain your integrity? How can you be a man of integrity in those situations?

5. How would you respond to someone who challenges the integrity of the Bible? How can you ready yourself for such a conversation?

Masculinity

Bible Passages

1. **1 Kings 2:1–4** – David to Solomon: "Show yourself a man."

2. **Job 40:1–9** – God to Job: "Gird up your loins like a man."

3. **Psalm 1** – A blessed man delights in God's law

4. **Psalm 4** – God sets apart men who follow Him

5. **John 2:13–22** – With a whip, Jesus cleanses the temple

6. **1 Corinthians 16:10–18** – Paul: "Act like men. Be strong."

7. **2 Peter 1:5–10** – A Christian brother has these qualities

Be watchful, stand firm in the faith, act like men, be strong.

—*1 Corinthians 16:13*

I was at a weekend men's retreat led by David Murrow, the author of *Why Men Hate Going to Church* and other books. Because I am friends with Murrow—and I gave him a lift to the retreat—he asked me to be his assistant for a few of his lessons.

The attendees were seated around five tables, with twelve to fifteen guys at each one. Murrow asked each table to select its strongest man. Five men came forward. "Now," Murrow announced, "we're going to find out who is the strongest man in the room." It would be a test of endurance. Who could do pushups, without more than a second in between, the longest?

Within two minutes, two men had quit. A minute later, a third dropped out, so it was down to two. These two men went at it for another minute. Then two. Then three. Finally, one of them could not lift his chest off the floor. He was done. We had a winner. Pointing to a chair, Murrow instructed the winner to sit on his "throne" in front of the rest of the men.

Then I zip-tied the man's wrists and ankles to the chair. "Let's see how strong you are now," said Murrow. "Get out of the chair!" The man made a mighty effort to break the zip-ties. He strained to pull his wrists up, to no avail. As he tried to move his legs, he flipped his chair (and himself) to the ground.

After we righted the chair, Murrow asked the room, "How is our strong man going to be freed? Can he struggle his way to freedom? Can he pray his way to freedom? What will it take to restore him to full strength?"

A man in the back shouted, "Anybody got a knife?" At that, I pulled out a pocketknife and freed our champion, and Murrow told the men in the room to explain what they had witnessed. In just a few minutes, they had the answers. Just as the strongest man in the room was unable to break free from the zip-ties, the strongest Christian can find himself unable to break free from sin on his own. He needs help from God . . . and support from his brothers.

The problem for many men is that they don't have a single Christian brother. They are attempting to follow Jesus without a man to walk beside them on the journey and, in most cases, without a good example of what it means to be a man of God.

In biblical times, the primary teacher of what it means to be a man of God—and what it means to be a man—was your dad. Fathers recognized that their every word and action was training for all their children, but especially for their sons. When David was about to die, he told his son Solomon, "Be strong, and show yourself a man, and keep the charge of the Lord your God, walking in his ways and keeping his statutes, his commandments, his rules, and his testimonies" (1 Kings 2:2–3). Later, Solomon wrote this advice to fathers: "Train up a child in the way he should go; even when he is old he will not depart from it" (Proverbs 22:6).

Today, about 25 percent of US boys are raised without a father in the home.[62] Vince Miller, founder of the men's ministry Resolute, writes, "As a man who has been fatherless almost all my life, I have found that defining masculinity is deceptively difficult. I didn't have someone around to demonstrate true and healthy manhood."[63] Even when fathers are around, they may be emotionally distant or have other flaws that make them poor models for healthy masculinity.

Jesus, of course, was not only the perfect man but also the perfect model of manhood. Consider just one overlooked aspect of Jesus: his toughness. Right after his baptism, Jesus went into the wilderness and fasted—for forty days! Then Satan tempted him, and Jesus, barely able to move or speak, resisted. Throughout his stressful three-year ministry—capped by an incredibly painful scourging and crucifixion—Jesus exhibited unparalleled physical and emotional toughness. And courage. And leadership. And humility. And love. And hundreds of other traits worth emulating.

To translate the example of Jesus to their own lives, men need help . . . from other men who, like they, are following Jesus.

The last day of the retreat was a Sunday. After a time of worship, the seventy participants decided to take Murrow's "strongest man" object lesson to heart. Each man put a zip tie on his wrist and agreed to wear it for a week. The next Sunday, in their home church, the men gathered together in front of the congregation. One explained the lesson to everyone in the room.

And then the men cut the zip ties off each other's wrists.

PRAYER

Jesus, you demonstrated how to be a man of God. I want to be such a man. Guide me and help me to find—or expand—my band of brothers. Amen.

Questions for Reflection and Application

1. Who have been your models for masculinity? Where have you followed their examples? Where have you chosen not to follow their examples, and why?

2. What types of men intimidate you, and why? What types of men do you think you intimidate, and why?

3. What masculine qualities of Jesus are undervalued in today's Christian church? Why?

4. In your opinion, what are the primary differences between "healthy masculinity" and "toxic masculinity"?

5. If you have Christian brothers who are walking beside you, then describe them and explain how they became your brothers in Christ. If you don't, then list the qualities that would make a man a good candidate to be your Christian brother and consider how you will befriend men with these qualities.

Politics

Bible Passages

1. **Daniel 2:17–24** – God sets up and removes kings

2. **Daniel 3** – Daniel's friends defy the king and are thrown into the fiery furnace

3. **Matthew 22:15–22** – Should we pay taxes to Caesar?

4. **Acts 5:27–33** – Peter and John must obey God rather than the ruling authorities

5. **Romans 13:1–7** – Submit to the authorities

6. **Philippians 3:17–21** – Our true citizenship is in heaven

7. **1 Timothy 2:1–7** – Pray for all, including rulers

. . . always being prepared to make a defense to anyone who asks you for a reason for the hope that is in you; yet do it with gentleness and respect, having a good conscience, so that, when you are slandered, those who revile your good behavior in Christ may be put to shame.

—*1 Peter 3:15b–16*

Our current world is not the way that it ought to be, says Joe Coffey, the lead pastor at Christ Community Chapel in Hudson, Ohio. Everyone has a hope in something that will move the world more toward what it was intended to be.

For some people, politics is their hope. "If we can just get the right people in office . . . If the government will just do what it's supposed to do . . . Then the world will be more of what we want it to be. What it was intended to be. More ideal."[64]

There certainly is nothing wrong with wanting a better world. More personal liberties. More equality. Less poverty. Fewer wars. Better healthcare. Less hunger. Better education. A cleaner environment. Stronger families. More opportunities.

Achieving these objectives requires the decisions and actions of government leaders. Influencing those leaders, and encouraging others to elect certain leaders, means getting involved in the political process. In today's world, however, it is easy to allow political engagement to overshadow our primary mission.

In *The Screwtape Letters,* an experienced demonic operative explains how a tempter can use politics to confuse a Christ-follower. The approach that Screwtape recommends is to start by treating a political goal as part of Christianity, then plant the idea that the goal is the most important part of one's religion. Finally, persuade the man that the chief value of Christianity is the excellent arguments it makes for the political goal.

"Once you have made the World an end, and faith as a means, you have almost won your man, and it makes very little difference what kind of worldly end he is pursuing," writes Screwtape. "Provided that meetings, pamphlets, policies, movements, causes, and crusades matter more to him than prayers and sacraments and charity, he is ours."[65]

How do you get involved in politics without losing sight of the bigger mission? How do you keep your priorities intact?

During the life of Jesus, all political discussions centered on the Romans, who controlled and ran all the land around the Mediterranean Sea, including the former kingdoms of Israel and Judah. To fund its empire, Rome levied taxes on every city and area under its rule. Every tax collector had to obtain a revenue target from his assigned jurisdiction. His "wage" was the difference between what he collected and his target.

Jews saw taxes as a tribute to Caesar, a hated despot who called himself a god, and a symbol of slavery to Rome. They believed that their messiah, or savior, would be a political leader who would overthrow Rome.

Would Jesus be that messiah? He taught with authority and exhibited amazing power. When he entered Jerusalem on the Sunday before Passover, a huge crowd hailed him as a king.

It was time to determine his intentions. The religious leaders approached him and asked him a test question: Is it lawful to pay taxes to Caesar, or not?

"Show me the coin for the tax," he responded. After they brought him a coin, he asked, "Whose likeness and inscription is this?" They said, "Caesar's." And Jesus said, "Therefore render to Caesar the things that are Caesar's, and to God the things that are God's."

He was not their political savior. He needed to go.

A few days later, Jesus was arrested and hauled in front of Pontius Pilate, the Roman governor who had the power to release Jesus or order his execution. "Are you the King of the Jews?" Pilate asked him. Jesus responded that he was, indeed, a king, but his kingdom was not of this world.

Christ offers each of us a place in his eternal kingdom. That realm is not threatened by the politics of our present world. But how we approach politics can threaten—or enhance—our witness to people who are not yet a part of that kingdom.

Political action can improve a part of this world and bring benefits to a segment of its population. But it will never make this world what it was intended to be, and it won't bring one person to his eternal destination.

Our hope remains in the One who can do both.

Let's act like it.

PRAYER

God, You command us to be *in* the world without being *of* the world. Forgive me when I care more about politics than about Your kingdom. Help me to keep my eyes on Jesus. Amen.

Questions for Reflection and Application

1. It's difficult to avoid political discussions. When someone presents a political viewpoint with which you disagree, how do you respond? Why?

2. How do you express Christian love to those with whom you disagree politically without compromising your principles?

3. How often do you pray for political leaders with whom you disagree? What do you say in those prayers?

4. The Bible instructs us to submit to the authorities, but there are many examples in the Bible where God's people resisted the authorities (such as Daniel 3). How do you know when to obey and when to disobey?

5. Is it possible to "stay out of politics" while still pursuing justice (see Micah 6:8)? If so, then how? If not, then what should your approach to politics be?

Pride

Bible Passages

1. **Psalm 10** – Pride causes a man to reject God

2. **Proverbs 16:1–6, 18–19** – God hates pride

3. **Isaiah 14:12–21** – God brings down the proud

4. **Luke 18:9–14** – Parable of the Pharisee and the tax collector

5. **2 Corinthians 4:5–12** – Everything good belongs to God

6. **James 4:1–10** – To combat pride, humble yourself before God

7. **1 Peter 5:5–6** – Humble yourself before God and others

But we have this treasure in jars of clay, to show that the surpassing power belongs to God and not to us.

—2 Corinthians 4:7

It was 1941. England had survived the Blitz, a series of massive German air attacks, but the cost had been great, with tens of thousands of civilians killed and a million houses destroyed or damaged. With the rattled British population preparing itself for a long and bloody war, the British Broadcasting Corporation (BBC) expanded its religious broadcasting to provide reassurance.

That expansion included some short talks by an Oxford fellow named C. S. Lewis, who had impressed BBC brass with his apologetic work, *The Problem of Pain*. Lewis's first two sets of talks focused on apologetics. For the third series, he shifted gears to cover Christian behavior, including "The Great Sin."

What is the great sin? What sin is worse than any other? It is the one of which every man is guilty, but most are unaware. No fault makes a man more unpopular; the more of it a man has in himself, the more he dislikes it in others. It is through this sin that the devil became the devil. This sin leads to every other vice; it is the complete anti-God state of mind. It is pride.

Recognizing that some in his audience would object to his premise, Lewis spent the rest of his talk giving reasons why pride is the worst of all sins.

A proud person has to be "better" than everyone else. "We say that people are proud of being rich, or clever, or good-looking, but they are not. They are proud of being richer, or cleverer, or better-looking than others. If someone else became equally rich, or clever, or good-looking there would be nothing to be proud about. It is the comparison that makes you proud: the pleasure of being above the rest."

A proud person is never satisfied. Competing with others is not always a sign of pride. For example, when resources are scarce, people often compete with each other for those resources. A proud person, however, will try to get more, even when he already has more than he needs. Many sins, such as greed and selfishness, are the result of pride, said Lewis.

A proud person craves power. Power, said Lewis, is what pride really enjoys. A proud person wants to feel superior, and power over others feeds a superiority complex. We can see the quest for power in everything from a beautiful woman who tries to amass admirers to a political leader who demands more influence and control. While other vices, such as drunkenness, sometimes bring people together, pride always drives people apart.

Pride makes you God's enemy. Pride not only makes people enemies with each other, it also makes people enemies with God. "In God you come up against something which is in every respect immeasurably superior to yourself. Unless you know God as that—and, therefore, know yourself as nothing in comparison—you do not know God at all. As long as you are proud you cannot know God. A proud man is always looking down on things and people: and, of course, as long as you are looking down, you cannot see something that is above you."

Pride makes you vulnerable to the devil. Vices other than pride, said Lewis, come from the devil working on us through our animal nature. Pride, on the other hand, is purely spiritual and, consequently, far more subtle and deadly. "Pride is spiritual cancer: it eats up the very possibility of love, or contentment, or even common sense."

You can be blind to your own pride. Lewis called vanity, or seeking and reveling in praise from others, the least bad type of pride. "The real black, diabolical Pride, comes when you look down on others so much that you do not care what they think of you." Or what God thinks of you.

Lewis's position on pride has plenty of biblical support. Solomon wrote, "Pride goes before destruction, and a haughty spirit before a fall" (Proverbs 16:18). James 4:6 and 1 Peter 5:5 have the same quote: "God opposes the proud but gives grace to the humble." And Jesus reserved his harshest criticism for the Pharisees, primarily because of their pride, as captured in his parable of the Pharisee and the tax collector (see Luke 18:9–14).

So how do we stop committing the Great Sin? How do we rid ourselves of pride? Obviously, we need to follow the example of Jesus, as explained in Philippians 2:5–11. But where do we start? The first step, Lewis said, is to admit that you struggle with pride. "If you don't think you are conceited," he said, "then you are very conceited indeed."[66]

PRAYER

Father, I confess that I struggle with pride. Create in me a clean heart and guide me to follow the example of Jesus. Amen.

Questions for Reflection and Application

1. What do you think of C. S. Lewis's contention that pride is the worst sin?
2. Where do you struggle the most with pride? Where is it not much of an issue for you?
3. What have been the consequences of your pride? How can you make amends for the impact of your pride on other people?
4. In what areas of life have you worked the hardest? What have you gained from that hard work? Do you give God just as much credit for what you have attained in those areas as you do in areas where you have not worked as hard? Why or why not?
5. Is it wrong to tell someone else that you are proud of him? Why or why not?
6. What is false modesty? In what areas of life is that a struggle for you? How can you overcome it?

Race

Bible Passages

1. **Genesis 1:26–27** – God made humankind in His image

2. **Luke 10:25–37** – The parable of the Good Samaritan

3. **John 4:1–43** – Jesus ministers in a Samaritan village

4. **Acts 8:4–25** – Philip takes the gospel to the Samaritans

5. **Acts 8:26–39** – Philip shares the gospel with an Ethiopian court official

6. **Acts 17:22–28** – God made all men from one man

7. **Revelation 7:9–17** – The multitude in heaven is from every nation, tribe, people, and language

But you are a chosen race, a royal priesthood, a holy nation, a people for his own possession, that you may proclaim the excellencies of him who called you out of darkness into his marvelous light.

—1 Peter 2:9

Jews hated Samaritans. And the feeling was mutual. It had been that way for centuries.

Back when the nation of Israel split in two—Israel to the north and Judah to the south—the capital of Israel was the city of Samaria. 250 years later, Israel was overpowered by the Assyrians. The conquerors sent tribes to live in Israel and intermarry with the Israelites. The hybrid people became the Samaritans.

Later, Judah was conquered by the Babylonians, and the best and brightest Jews were exiled to Babylon. Many of them intermarried with foreigners, but some did not. When the Persian King Cyrus allowed Jews to return to their homeland, only the most devout Jews did so, with the purpose of rebuilding Jerusalem and its temple. The Jews who returned were zealous for God and the Scriptures. Scribes copied the Scriptures, and synagogues and schools were established to teach from them.

Meanwhile, the Samaritans developed their own version of Judaism. They had their own Pentateuch (the first five books) in Aramaic, which differed from the Hebrew Pentateuch, and they did not accept the other books of the Hebrew Scriptures. They also had different worship practices. After the Jews rejected the Samaritan offer to help rebuild the Jerusalem temple (see Ezra 4) and exiled a high priest's brother for marrying a Samaritan, the Samaritans built their own temple on Mount Gerizim.

Samaritans saw themselves as the true Israelites and keepers of the covenant. Jews saw Samaritans as "half-bloods" who were not welcome in the kingdom of heaven.

After Jewish communities were established north of Samaria in Galilee, some Jews sought to settle on Samaritan land. Border skirmishes ensued. After Jews destroyed the Samaritan temple, Samaritans responded by harassing and even killing Jews who traveled between Galilee and Jerusalem. Galileans began to add days to their journey to and from Jerusalem to avoid Samaria.[67]

A Samaritan village once rejected Jesus simply because he was a Jewish rabbi traveling from Galilee to Jerusalem. When James and John asked Jesus if they should call down heavenly fire to consume that village, Jesus rebuked them, and they went to another village (see Luke 9:51-55).

The story was very different when Jesus and his disciples came to the Samaritan town of Sychar. Jesus sat down beside a well around noon. When a woman came to draw water, Jesus asked her for a drink. "How is it that you, a Jew, ask for a drink from me, a woman of Samaria?" she asked. As they began to converse, Jesus revealed that he knew everything about her. She responded by asking him a religious question: is the true temple in Jerusalem or Samaria? That really doesn't matter, Jesus replied, because God is spirit, and true worship is in spirit and truth.

After the conversation, the woman ran throughout Sychar, saying that she had met the Messiah. As a result, many Samaritans from the town came to Jesus—a Jew—and asked him to stay with them. After two days, many more believed and professed that Jesus was "the Savior of the world" (see John 4).

Another time, Jesus told ten lepers to show themselves to the priests. They were healed on the way, but only one, a Samaritan, returned to thank Jesus. "Your faith has made you well," said Jesus (see Luke 17:11-19).

Clearly, Samaritans were welcome in the kingdom. But Jesus went one step—a huge step—further in a famous parable, which was told in response to a lawyer's question: Who is my neighbor?

In the parable, a Jew traveling to Jericho is robbed, stripped, beaten, and left for dead. A priest, and then a Levite, see him and travel on. Then a Samaritan, deep in Jewish territory, arrives. The Samaritan has compassion on the Jew, binds up his wounds, takes him all the way to an inn, and stays with him overnight. The next day, he pays the innkeeper to care for the man and vows to return and cover any additional expenses.

"Which of these three, do you think, proved to be a neighbor to the man who fell among the robbers?" asked Jesus. The lawyer, unwilling to say the word "Samaritan," replied, "The one who showed him mercy." Jesus said, "You go, and do likewise."

PRAYER

Almighty God, You made each of us in Your image. Guide me to treat everyone as my equal, regardless of his race or ethnicity. Amen.

Questions for Reflection and Application

1. How many of your close friends are men of a race that is different from yours? Why is that? How would you expand your friend "circle" to include more men of different races?

2. How do you demonstrate your feelings and beliefs on race in your conversations? Statements online? Actions?

3. In 1960, Martin Luther King, Jr. called 11 a.m. on Sunday morning the most segregated hour in Christian America. How much have things changed since 1960? Is the fact that the worshippers at most churches are primarily of one race due to racism among Christians? What are other potential causes of this phenomenon?

4. What should be your role in achieving more racial harmony in your community? How are you doing?

5. Many Jews in America consider themselves to be ethnic Jews rather than devout practitioners of Judaism. How many of your close friends are ethnic Jews? Why is that? How would you expand your friend "circle" to include more ethnic Jews?

Social Justice

Bible Passages

1. **Psalm 146** – God helps those who need His help

2. **Proverbs 31:6–9** – Defend rights of the poor and needy

3. **Isaiah 1:16–20** – Seek justice for the weak and oppressed

4. **Amos 5:11–15** – God does not bless those who hurt the poor and needy

5. **Micah 6:6–8** – What does God require of you?

6. **Matthew 25:31–46** – A righteous man ministers to the needy

7. **1 John 3:16–18** – Demonstrate love in deed and in truth

"Blessed are those who hunger and thirst for righteousness, for they shall be satisfied."

—Matthew 5:6

As a teenager, William Booth saw first-hand the sheer poverty and oppression of England's working-class masses. He also found saving faith at the Broad Street Wesley Chapel in Nottingham. Soon after his conversion, Booth helped conduct evangelical street meetings and brought new converts to the Broad Street Chapel. When Booth's rag-tag bunch sat in pews reserved for the wealthy parishioners, church leaders told Booth to bring the poor through the back door and seat them in more obscure pews. That rebuke helped shape Booth's future.

Over the next decade, Booth's dynamic and even sensational methods of preaching, including on street corners in the slums, led thousands to confess faith in Christ. He became a fully ordained minister in the Methodist Church, but his church duties prevented him from working in the "Cathedral of the Open Air." When the denomination refused to release him from his regular circuit work, Booth and his wife left the Methodist Church and, in 1861, began conducting evangelical rallies all over England.

Booth's rallies led to the forming of a chain of missions, eventually called The Salvation Army. While Booth provided spiritual nourishment, the missions provided for the physical needs of the poor. By 1879, the Army had eighty-one stations, 127 full-time evangelists (mostly Booth's converts), and 75,000 services a year. The following year it expanded to the United States, where it provided ice carts in the summer, coal wagons in the winter, and salvage crews, soup kitchens, rescue homes, employment bureaus, hospitals, shelters, and thrift shops all year round.

Today, The Salvation Army, which describes itself as "an integral part of the Christian Church," operates in over 130 countries and claims that it is "the world's largest nongovernmental provider of poverty relief, serving more than 23 million in need each year in America alone." The Army's slogan—"Heart to God & Hand to Man"—reflects the goal of advancing Christianity while providing for society's downtrodden through "education, the relief of poverty, and other charitable objects."[68]

Booth's mission was to bring salvation, and hope, to the poor in England. Branch Rickey's mission was to provide opportunities for blacks in America's cherished, and segregated, pastime: baseball.

Rickey played four years in the majors, but he was cut by the Cincinnati Reds because he refused to play games on Sundays. So, he decided to get his law degree, and coach baseball, at the University of Michigan. When the team played a weekend series at Notre Dame, the hotel refused to allow the team's best player, a black man, to stay there. "Put him in with me," Rickey told the hotel manager. The hotel accommodated his request.

After Michigan, Rickey worked his way up the ladder at several major league teams. In 1945, as Brooklyn Dodgers president, he decided that it was time to desegregate baseball. When scouts identified Jackie Robinson as a black player with major league potential, Rickey met with him and offered him a contract. At that meeting, Rickey explained that Robinson would face constant bigotry and would not be able to fight back. Knowing that Robinson was a Christian, Rickey challenged him to turn the other cheek as Jesus had instructed. Robinson vowed to do so.

In 1946, playing for the Dodgers' minor league affiliate, Robinson was named the league's Most Valuable Player. The next spring, Rickey announced that Robinson would open the season as the Brooklyn Dodgers' first baseman. The Dodgers went on to win the National League championship that year, and Robinson was named Rookie of the Year. Robinson's success led other baseball owners to seek talented black players, and by 1952 there were 150 blacks playing in organized baseball.

After spearheading the fight against racial injustice in baseball, Rickey spent the rest of his life lending his vocal support to civil rights in other areas of American life.[69]

The first century Jews whom Jesus taught worshipped a God of justice. The Hebrew word for justice, *mishpat*, could mean punishment for wrongdoing, but it also could mean treating people, especially vulnerable people, fairly. In Psalm 146, for example, God executes *mishpat* for the oppressed, not the guilty. And Micah 6:8 says this: "He has told you, O man, what is good; and what does the Lord require of you but to do *mishpat*, and to love kindness, and to walk humbly with your God?"

Booth and Rickey followed God's call for *mishpat*. So can you.

PRAYER

God, I am your servant, a part of Christ's body on earth. Lead me to bring justice and mercy to those who need it. Amen.

Questions for Reflection and Application

1. Describe your personal experience, or the experiences of friends, with being "poor and needy." What are some ways that you can gain insight into other people's needs for *mishpat*?

2. God commands us to serve him not just with our treasure (financial contributions) but also with our time and our talents. How are you using all three to assist the needy, especially those in your community?

3. Which opportunities to assist the needy in your community provide the best "fit" for your abilities and experience? How can you pursue those opportunities?

4. Social justice has become a politically charged topic. How can you pursue social justice without alienating those who disagree with you on the role of government in administering social justice?

Theology

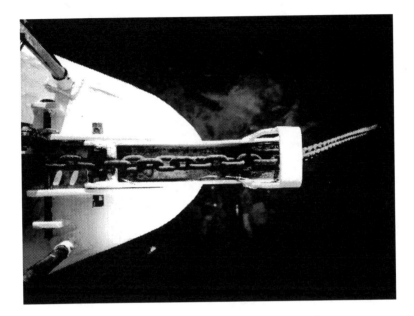

Bible Passages

1. **Psalm 119** – David praises God's Word
2. **Isaiah 40:6–8** – The Word of God stands forever
3. **John 1:1–18** – Jesus is the Word made flesh
4. **1 Timothy 6:3–5** – Teach sound doctrine
5. **2 Timothy 3:1–13** – Godlessness in the last days
6. **1 Peter 1:22–25** – The gospel is the Word of God
7. **2 Peter 3:14–18** – Peter vouches for Paul

All Scripture is breathed out by God and profitable for teaching, for reproof, for correction, and for training in righteousness, that the man of God may be complete, equipped for every good work.

—2 Timothy 3:16–17

Shortly after the death and resurrection of Jesus, 3,000 men became Christians in one day. As Peter, Paul, and other apostles preached the gospel, the number of believers swelled.

Then persecutions began. The apostles and other eyewitnesses of Jesus were killed. A Jewish uprising led to a bloody siege in Jerusalem; when it was over, the city that was the epicenter of both Judaism and Christianity lay in rubble, its population nearly wiped out. By the beginning of the second century, there may have been fewer than 10,000 Christians left . . . anywhere. If those remaining were arrested and refused to recant their faith, they were executed.

As if persecutions were not enough, the "Jesus movement" faced an even greater threat: subversion from within. Some who claimed to be Christians said that Jesus was not God, or that recent prophecies superseded the apostles' teachings. The most serious heresy was Gnosticism, which claimed that Jesus was not human but a spirit person who taught that secret spiritual knowledge (gnosis) was the gateway to salvation. Gnostic writings sounded biblical, but they undercut the foundation of the church: creeds (unifying statements of belief), the Old Testament, and the apostles' teachings (the New Testament).[70]

To avoid being swept away by compelling heresies, early Christians needed to anchor their faith on a sound theology—a sound biblical understanding of the nature of God and of truth. We need that same anchor, argues author Lee Strobel, to combat a modern-day heresy: "the false gospel that so many 'progressive' Christian leaders are espousing."[71]

Progressive Christians, of course, disagree. They identify as Christians who are "progressing" in their knowledge, understanding, and spirituality, even if that "progress" results in rejecting tenets of orthodox Christianity such as the inerrancy of Scripture, the existence of hell, and salvation by atonement. "Tradition, dogma, and doctrine are all fair game," writes John Pavlovitz. God is not "landlocked to a 6,000-year-old collection of writings," and Christian tradition is embedded with "misogyny, racism, anti-Semitism, and homophobia." The heart of the gospel, and the central work of Jesus, is not salvation; it is social justice.[72]

Many of today's popular Christian authors, bloggers, and speakers are progressive. Progressive ideology has become mainstream in many seminaries, denominations, and churches.

Having grown up "witnessing the gospel in action," Alisa Childers considered herself a strong Christian until she participated in a discussion group with a progressive Christian pastor. Over the course of a few months, the pastor systematically dismantled various tenets of her faith that she had never questioned. Childers was "thrust into a spiritual blackout." For the first time, she was forced to wrestle with why she believed certain things. Her faith had been deconstructed. She had to reconstruct it.

On her journey of reconstruction, she found ample evidence that Christianity is "deeply rooted in history" and that "the core historic claims of Christianity are true." Today's Christians can use the same ammunition that equipped the earliest followers.[73]

Take 1 Corinthians 15:3–5. Scholars, even skeptics, say that this creed began circulating within two to seven years of Jesus's resurrection. Followers of Jesus professed that he lived, he died for our sins, he was buried, he rose from the dead, and he appeared to eyewitnesses who, at the time the creed was first spoken, were alive and could be consulted for corroboration. Further, the creed says that the life, atoning death, burial, and resurrection of Jesus were foretold in the Jewish Scriptures (Old Testament) and therefore were inseparable from those Scriptures.

Several other early creeds affirm the deity of Jesus. So too does an early hymn, which Paul records in Philippians 2:6–11. Paul wrote Philippians about thirty years after the death and resurrection of Jesus, so the hymn obviously was sung earlier.

The core tenets of our faith were professed before any of the New Testament was written. The apostles and other eyewitnesses of the risen Jesus refused to renounce their faith, even when they were killed for being followers of Jesus.

Let's keep the anchor of our faith secure. With a grounded faith, we can throw a lifeline to those who are caught in a current. Any current.

PRAYER

God, I need You to be my anchor, so that I can withstand the storms of life. Show me the way. Amen.

Questions for Reflection and Application

1. What are the anchors of your faith? Why are these your anchors? How have they been tested?

2. What are your views on progressive Christianity and its theology?

3. Christians in the early church in Berea were considered "noble" because they tested the (spoken) gospel message against the Scriptures, or what we call the Old Testament today (see Acts 17:10–15). How do you test the Christian messages that you read and hear? How confident are you in your ability to test these messages?

4. Protestant Christianity places less stock in the traditions of the Christian church than do Roman Catholicism and Orthodox Christianity. What are some of the potential benefits of Christian traditions? What are some of the potential downsides?

Wealth

Bible Passages

1. **Matthew 6:19–24** – Store up riches in heaven

2. **Matthew 19:16–30** – It is difficult for a rich person to enter the kingdom of God

3. **Matthew 25:14–30** – Give God a return on His investment

4. **Luke 12:13–21** – The parable of the rich fool

5. **Luke 16:10–15, 19–31** – You cannot serve God and money

6. **Acts 4:32–35** – Early Christians shared everything

7. **1 Timothy 6:6–10** – The love of money is the root of all kinds of evil

Jesus said to him, "If you would be perfect, go, sell what you possess and give to the poor, and you will have treasure in heaven; and come, follow me."

—Matthew 19:21

H is family was rich. One of the wealthiest in Jerusalem. It had been that way for generations.

The wealth brought him power. And respect. He was a Pharisee, but not an ordinary Pharisee. His wealth put him in a different class, making him one of a select few powerful and distinguished aristocrats who, together with the chief priests, ran things in Jerusalem, answering only to the Romans. And he was a rabbi. Not all Pharisees were, but he was revered as a teacher of the law. More power. More prestige.

Then Jesus came on the scene. Nicodemus sensed that the young rabbi was more than a rabbi. A prophet, maybe. Maybe more. But Jesus was also a threat to the established order, and he had the potential to put all that Nicodemus possessed at risk. Nicodemus needed more information. So, he arranged for a private meeting with Jesus. At night.

Jesus opened the conversation by dropping a bomb: No one—not even a wealthy and respected Jewish ruler and teacher of the law—would enter the kingdom of God unless he was born again.

Born again? Nicodemus had no idea what that meant. Jesus explained that it was a birth of water and the Spirit, but that didn't help. Nicodemus remained completely baffled. Jesus poked him with this: "Are you the teacher of Israel and yet you do not understand these things?"

That would have made other Pharisees furious. Not Nicodemus. He trusted his gut, and he signaled for Jesus to continue. So Jesus revealed his true identity: the Son of Man. Descended from heaven. Here on a mission: "For God so loved the world, that he gave his only Son, that whoever believes in him should not perish but have eternal life. For God did not send his Son into the world to condemn the world, but in order that the world might be saved through him."

When Jesus finished, Nicodemus realized that he was straddling two worlds. In one, his wealth meant everything. In the other, his wealth meant nothing. He didn't want to leave the first world. Not yet. So he devised a way to live in both worlds: he would keep his allegiance to Jesus a secret.

That seemed to work, for a while. But Jesus would not allow the scheme to continue. He took on the teachers of the law and left them in the dust. He confronted the ruling elite and won every confrontation. And then he started to turn the people against them.

The chief priests and Pharisees sent officers to arrest Jesus. When the officers returned empty-handed, the Pharisees said that they, like the crowd, had been deceived by Jesus. "Have any of the authorities or the Pharisees believed in him?" they asked.

Nicodemus had. But he couldn't reveal that to them. Maybe if they could talk to Jesus, as he had, then they would change their minds. "Does our law judge a man without first giving him a hearing and learning what he does?" he asked his fellow elites.

Their response mocked him. "Are you from Galilee too?"

He could not live in both worlds. If he admitted that he was a follower of Jesus, then he would lose his wealth and all that came with it. He would no longer be a powerful and respected leader. He would be a Galilean. Just like Jesus.

Soon, the Jewish rulers succeeded in having Jesus arrested. Twelve hours later, he was hanging on a cross, dying of blood loss from the scourging he had received. By mid-afternoon, he was dead.

Nicodemus then made his choice. In full daylight, he and another Pharisee, Joseph of Arimathea, along with their servants, gave Jesus, a man killed as a criminal, a burial befitting a king. A few days later, Nicodemus realized that Jesus was the true King.

Christian tradition and apocryphal works hold that Nicodemus was baptized by Peter and John and discovered the high cost of being a disciple of Jesus. Nicodemus suffered persecution from hostile Jews, lost his membership in the Sanhedrin, and was forced to leave Jerusalem. It is believed that, in the fifth century, the remains of Nicodemus were found in a grave alongside the remains of Stephen.[74]

They, like all other followers of Jesus, are promised wealth that far exceeds anything we can amass on this terrestrial ball.

PRAYER

God, You have given me so much. I want to make the most of it—not for myself but for You and Your kingdom. Guide me so that I avoid the many pitfalls that money can bring. Amen.

Questions for Reflection and Application

1. In the time of Jesus, wealth was considered a sign of God's blessings. Why did Jesus speak out so often and so strongly against amassing wealth?
2. Jesus said that it is easier for a camel to go through the eye of a needle than for a rich man to enter the kingdom of God. How do you feel about that statement?
3. What is your current financial situation? Are you where you want to be financially? Why or why not?
4. Describe your approach to managing your finances. Why do you have that approach? How has it changed over time?
5. Who have been your mentors in the area of financial management? How do (or how did) they manage their money?
6. What are the key differences between sound financial planning (to provide for your needs and those of your loved ones) and amassing too much wealth?
7. What does God want you to do in the area of money?

Day 365

Fifty-two weeks is 364 days. In case this book is marketed as a complete one-year devotional, it needs one more day of material, so I'm providing that here. (The marketing team has not advised me on what to do if you read this book during a leap year.)

My primary goal for this devotional is to get you reading your Bible, because regular Bible reading brings at least four benefits:

1. **It draws you closer to God.** The primary way that God reveals Himself to us is through the Bible. The more you read the Bible, the better you get to know God, and the more you want to communicate with Him and follow Him.
2. **The Bible is the perfect handbook for daily living.** It includes wisdom, commandments that provide sound rules for living, the rationale behind those commandments, and stories of the consequences of not following God.
3. **Reading the Bible regularly improves your behavior.** Research by the Center for Bible Engagement reveals that the frequency with which you read your Bible is a more reliable prediction of moral behavior than traditional measures of spirituality, such as church attendance and prayer.
4. **The Bible encourages and strengthens you.** When life gets you down, you need comfort. Reassurance. Strength. Peace. Hope. Whatever you need, and whenever you need it, the Bible supplies it by reminding you that God created you in His image and loves you deeply.

So, how are you going to stay consistent in your Bible reading over the next year? I guess you can do this devotional again. Or another one, even one that wasn't written by me. Or you can get a Bible reading plan.

Whatever way you read your Bible, read it with a friend. He will give you insights that you probably wouldn't have on your own. He also will keep you accountable and give you encouragement. Besides, teaming up is biblical; see Ecclesiastes 4:9–12, Matthew 18:20, Mark 6:7, and Luke 10:1.

The Bible is a very good gift from a very good God.

Endnotes

1. The scenes are from the film *Witness* (1985), written by Earl W. Wallace and William Kelley, directed by Peter Weir.

2. Kenneth E. Bailey, *The Cross and the Prodigal: Luke 15 Through the Eyes of Middle Eastern Peasants* (IVP Books, 2005).

3. Robert J. Morgan, *Then Sings My Soul: 150 of the World's Greatest Hymn Stories* (Thomas Nelson, 2003); David Sheward, "The Real Story Behind 'Amazing Grace'," Biography.com, August 11, 2015; and other online sources.

4. Bradley J. Birzer, "Mark Hollis: Rest Your Head," *The Imaginative Conservative*, theimaginativeconservative.org/2019/02/mark-hollis-rest-your-head-bradley-birzer.html; Daniel Kreps, "Talk Talk's Mark Hollis Dead at 64," *Rolling Stone*, February 26, 2019; and Adrian Deevoy, "Talk Talk: 'You should never listen to music as background music'—a classic interview from the vaults," *The Guardian*, August 28, 2013.

5. "Seasonal Affective Disorder: What You Should Know," Johns Hopkins Medicine website, www.hopkinsmedicine.org/health/conditions-and-diseases/seasonal-affective-disorder-what-you-should-know; and "Seasonal affective disorder: Bring on the Light," Harvard University Health website, www.health.harvard.edu/blog/seasonal-affective-disorder-bring-on-the-light-201212215663.

6. Robert Barron, "Recovering the Strangeness of Easter," *The Wall Street Journal* (April 2, 2021).

7. Robert J. Morgan, *Then Sings My Soul: 150 of the World's Greatest Hymn Stories* (Thomas Nelson, 2003); and William J. Petersen and Ardyth Petersen, *The Complete Book of Hymns* (Tyndale House Publishers, 2006).

8. Bob Simon, correspondent, "Saving the Children," *60 Minutes*, April 27, 2014.

9. Charles Dickens, *A Christmas Carol*, 1843.

10. Anna Wierzbicka, *What Christians Believe: The Story of God and People in Minimal English* (Oxford University Press, 2019); and Archpriest Oleg Stenyayev, "Pontius Pilate's Wife," Orthodox Christianity website, orthochristian.com/102542 .html.

11. Some scholars question whether or not the disciple and apostle Peter wrote 2 Peter. There is strong evidence that he did, including information from *The Catholic Encyclopedia* referenced at christianforums.com/threads/what-is-the-evidence-of-peter -in-rome.7336954/.

12. The dialog is from the film *Thor: Ragnarok* (2017), written by Eric Pearson and Craig Kyle & Christopher L. Yost, directed by Taika Waititi.

13. Stephen A. Diamond, PhD, "The Primacy of Anger Problems," *Psychology Today*, January 18, 2009.

14. The scenes and dialog are from the film *Silverado* (1985), written by Lawrence Kasdan and Mark Kasdan, directed by Lawrence Kasdan.

15. Kyle Idleman, *not a fan.: Becoming a Completely Committed Follower of Jesus* (Zondervan, 2011).

16. James Freeman, "The Hockey Team That Beat the Soviets— and the 1970s Malaise," *The Wall Street Journal*, February 21, 2020; and Dane Mizutani, "'Again!' An oral history of Herb Brooks' (in)famous bag skate in Norway," *Twin Cities Pioneer Press*, February 20, 2020.

17. Dr. Henry Cloud and Dr. John Townsend, *Boundaries: When to Say Yes, How to Say No to Take Control of Your Life* (Zondervan, 1992).

18. Brandon Showalter, "John Piper: Difference Between God's Judgement and Discipline Is 'Infinite'," *Christian Post*, February 13, 2017.

19. Paul Newman, "Revealed: The diet that saved Novak Djokovic," *The Independent*, July 1, 2019.

20. Chris Bolinger, "How Churches Can Address the National Issue of Fatherlessness," Crosswalk.com website, crosswalk.com /church/pastors-or-leadership/how-churches-can-address-the -national-issue-of-fatherlessness.html.

21. The scenes and dialog are from the film *Parenthood* (1989), written by Lowell Ganz, Babaloo Mandel, and Ron Howard, directed by Ron Howard.

22. Clare Bruce, "Christians with Anxiety? It's More Common Than You Think," Hope 103.2 website, hope1032.com.au/stori es/life/health-and-fitness/2019/christians-with-anxiety-its-mo re-common-than-you-think/.

23. "Marriage and Couples," The Gottman Institute website, gottman.com/about/research/couples/; and Zach Brittle, "L is for Love & Like," The Gottman Institute website, gottman.com /blog/l-is-for-love-like/.

24. Dr. Emerson Eggerichs, *Love and Respect: The Love She Most Desires; The Respect He Desperately Needs* (Thomas Nelson, 2004); and the Love and Respect website (loveandrespect.com /about-us).

25. Kenneth Osbeck, *101 Hymn Stories* (Kregel Publications, 1982).

26. Steve Riach, *Heart of a Champion* (B & H Pub Group, 2001); and "Kurt Warner," Biography.com, biography.com/peop le/kurt-warner-519490.

27. Ramona Shelburne, "John Lindsey waits for his chance," ESPN.com, August 29, 2010, espn.com/los-angeles/mlb/colu mns/story?id=5510887; "John Lindsay," Kazan Today website, kazantoday.com/WeeklyArticles/john-lindsey.html; and John Lindsey entry on the Minor League Baseball website, milb.com /player/index.jsp?player_id=439664.

28. C. S. Lewis, *The Problem of Pain* (1940).

29. "Helen Joy Davidman," Geni.com website, geni.com/peop le/Helen-Joy-Davidman/6000000010556089422.

30. C. S. Lewis, *A Grief Observed* (1961).

31. The dialog is from the film *The Terminator* (1984), written by James Cameron and Gale Anne Hurd, directed by James Cameron.

32. Paul Vigna, "Job satisfaction among American workers continues to increase, but there are more reasons than salary: poll," *The Patriot News*, September 2, 2019.

33. Ryan Nelson, "How Did the Apostles Die? What We Actually Know," OverviewBible.com, December 17, 2019, overvi ewbible.com/how-did-the-apostles-die/.

34. Andrew Rawnsley, "Appeasing Hilter by Tim Bouverie review—how Britain fell for a delusion," *The Guardian*, April 14, 2019; Christopher Klein, "Chamberlain Declares 'Peace for Our Time'," History.com, updated January 3, 2020; and Malcolm Gladwell, *Talking to Strangers: What We Should Know about the People We Don't Know* (Confer Books, 2019).

35. C. S Lewis, *The Screwtape Letters* (preface to 1961 edition).

36. The scenes and dialog are from *The Matrix* (1999), written by Lilly Wachowski and Lana Wachowski, directed by Lana Wachowski and Lilly Wachowski.

37. David Instone-Brewer, *Church Doctrine and the Bible: Theology in Ancient Context* (Lexham Press, 2020).

38. Lewis B. Smedes, *Forgive and Forget: Healing the Hurts We Don't Deserve* (Harper, 1984).

39. The scenes and dialog are from the film *Spider-Man 3* (2007), screenplay by Sam Raimi, Ivan Raimi, and Alvin Sargent, directed by Sam Raimi.

40. Catherine Yang, "Why Music Reminds Us We Are Human, Even in the Darkest Places," *The Epoch Times*, February 23, 2021, theepochtimes.com/edition/life-tradition-weekly-8-2_3705913 /3646216.

41. William Pierson Merrill, "Rise up, O men of God," 1911.

42. "Pharisee," *Encyclopedia Britannica*, britannica.com/topic /Pharisee; and N. T. Wright, *The New Testament in Its World: An Introduction to the History, Literature, and Theology of the First Christians* (Zondervan Academic, 2019).

43. Charles E. Hummel, *Tyranny of the Urgent* (IVP Books, 1967, 1994).

44. Harriet Constable, "Sheep are not stupid, and they are not helpless either," BBC.com, April 19, 2017, and Tamsin Cooper, "How Smart Are Sheep? Researchers Find Surprising Answers," Countryside.com, October 27, 2020, iamcountryside.com/sheep /how-smart-are-sheep/.

45. "Turkish sheep die in 'mass jump'," BBC News, July 8, 2005, news.bbc.co.uk/2/hi/europe/4665511.stm.

46. Bruce Wilkinson, *Secrets of the Vine: Breaking Through to Abundance* (Multnomah, 2001).

47. The scenes and dialog are from the film *Field of Dreams* (1989), screenplay by Phil Alden Robinson (based on a book by W. P. Kinsella), directed by Phil Alden Robinson.

48. "Core conditioning—It's not just about abs," Harvard Health Publishing online, May 22, 2012, health.harvard.edu/he althbeat/core-conditioning-its-not-just-about-abs; and Brittany Hambleton, "The importance of core strength for runners," *Canadian Running*, April 6, 2021.

49. William Shakespeare, *Henry V*, Act 4, Scene 3.

50. Sarah Pruitt, "What Went Wrong on Apollo 13?" History.com, April 13, 2020, history.com/news/apollo-13-what-went-wrong; "The Apollo 13 Flight Journal," NASA website, history.nasa.gov/afj/ap13fj/; and George Leopold, "Power engineer: Video interview with Apollo astronaut Ken Mattingly," *EE Times*, March 17, 2009, eetimes.com/power-engineer-video-interview-with-apollo-astronaut-ken-mattingly/.

51. Isaac Watts, "O God, Our Help in Ages Past," 1719.

52. The scenes and dialog are from the films *Galaxy Quest* (1999), written by David Howard and Robert Gordon, directed by Dean Parisot; *Back to the Future* (1985), written by Robert Zemeckis and Bob Gale, directed by Robert Zemeckis; and *Avengers: Endgame* (2019), written by Christopher Markus and Stephen McFeely, directed by Anthony Russo and Joe Russo.

53. William J. Petersen and Ardyth Petersen, *The Complete Book of Hymns* (Tyndale House Publishers, 2006); and Robert J. Morgan, *Then Sings My Soul: 150 of the World's Greatest Hymn Stories* (Thomas Nelson, 2003).

54. Author's interview with Dan Gregory, 2021.

55. "Benjamin Franklin's last great quote and the Constitution," National Constitution Center's Constitution Daily blog, constitutioncenter.org/blog/benjamin-franklins-last-great-quote-and-the-constitution/.

56. Janet Kinosian, "Pilgrim's Progress: Billy Graham on Death, Dying And Faith," HuffPost Contributor platform, November 17, 2011, huffpost.com/entry/pilgrims-progress-billy-g_b_472137.

57. David Instone-Brewer, *Divorce and Remarriage in the Church: Biblical Solutions for Pastoral Realities* (IVP Books, 2006); and Chris Bolinger, "4 Critical Insights On Divorce and Its Effect On Men," Crosswalk.com website, March 26, 2019, crosswalk.com/faith/men/4-critical-insights-on-divorce-and-its-effect-on-men.html.

58. Allan Turner, "Boxer-turned-preacher George Foreman is pastor at Houston Church," *Houston Chronicle*, August 11, 2015.

59. Ron Borges, "He Has a Higher Calling: Byner Finds Religion and Pro Bowl Success," *Boston Globe*, January 11, 1991; and a (very difficult to watch) video replay of the 1988 AFC Championship Game.

60. Rick Wade, "Persecution in the Early Church," Probe Ministries website, May 27, 1999, probe.org/persecution-in-the -early-church, and numerous sources cited in that article.

61. The scenes and dialog are from the film *The Untouchables* (1987), written by David Mamet (based on the book by Oscar Fraley and Eliot Ness), directed by Brian De Palma.

62. Table: "Child population by household type in the United States," KIDS COUNT data center: A project of the Annie E. Casey Foundation, datacenter.kidscount.org/data/tables/105 -child-population-by-household-type.

63. Vince Miller, "Nine Attributes of a Real Man," desiringGod website, October 15, 2016, desiringgod.org/articles/nine-attribu tes-of-a-real-man.

64. Joe Coffey sermon: "Reimagine (Part 2): Every Community," Christ Community Chapel (Hudson, Ohio), October 2020.

65. C. S. Lewis, *The Screwtape Letters*, 1942.

66. George M. Marsden, *C. S. Lewis's Mere Christianity: A Biography* (Princeton University Press, 2016); C. S. Lewis, *Mere Christianity*, 1952; and the C. S. Lewis website, cslewis.com.

67. James M. Rochford, "History of the Samaritans," Evidence Unseen website, www.evidenceunseen.com/theology/historical -theology/history-of-the-samaritans/, and other online sources.

68. Author's interview with staff members of The Salvation Army, 2019.

69. Pat Williams, *Triumph!: Powerful Stories of Athletes of Faith* (Barbour Publishing, 2014); and "Branch Rickey," Biography .com, biography.com/people/branch-rickey-9458118.

70. Jeffrey L. Sheler, "Days of the Martyrs," *U.S. News & World Report*, April 16, 2001; and Simonetta Carr, "Irenaeus of Lyon," *Christianity Today*, June 16, 2019.

71. Alisa Childers, *Another Gospel?: A Lifelong Christian Seeks Truth in Response to Progressive Christianity* (Tyndale Momentum, 2020).

72. John Pavlovitz, "Progressive Christianity—is Christianity," John Pavlovitz blog, October 5, 2016, johnpavlovitz.com/2016/10/05/explaining-progressive-christianity-otherwise-known-as-christianity.

73. Alisa Childers, *Another Gospel?: A Lifelong Christian Seeks Truth in Response to Progressive Christianity* (Tyndale Momentum, 2020).

74. Scenes and dialog are from John 3:1-21, 7:32-52, and 19:38-42; extrabiblical information on Nicodemus comes primarily from "Nicodemus and the Gurion family," The Free Library, www.thefreelibrary.com/Nicodemus+and+the+Gurion+family.-a0156735378 (Oxford University Press, 1996).

Printed in the United States
by Baker & Taylor Publisher Services